Springer Series on Social Work

Albert R. Roberts, D.S.W., Series Editor
School of Social Work, Indiana University, Indianapolis

Advisory Board: Joseph D. Anderson, D.S.W., Barbara Berkman, D.S.W., Paul H. Ephross, Ph.D., Sheldon R. Gelman, Ph.D., Nancy A. Humphreys, D.S.W., Sheldon Siegel, Ph.D., and Julia Watkins, Ph.D.

Hans S. Falck, Ph.D., F.R.S.H., is a professor of social work at the School of Social Work and professor of psychiatry at the Medical College of Virginia, both of Virginia Commonwealth University in Richmond. He is the chair of the Health Specialization in the School of Social Work. Dr. Falck is a widely published author of articles and monographs and from 1978 until 1984 was editor of the *Journal of Education for Social Work.* In addition to his studies in social work, he continues to work in neuroscience research with particular emphasis on the role of neurotransmitters as contributors to normal human behavior. He is a Fellow of the Royal Society of Health (London).

Social Work
The Membership
Perspective

Hans S. Falck, Ph.D.

Foreword by
Thomas Owen Carlton, D.S.W.

SPRINGER PUBLISHING COMPANY
New York

Copyright © 1988 by Springer Publishing Company, Inc.

All rights reserved

No part of this publication may be reproduced, stored in a retrieval system, or transmitted in any form or by any means, electronic, mechanical, photocopying, recording, or otherwise, without the prior permission of Springer Publishing Company, Inc.

Springer Publisher Company, Inc.
536 Broadway
New York, NY 10012
88 89 90 91 92 / 5 4 3 2 1

LIBRARY OF CONGRESS
Library of Congress Cataloging-in-Publication Data

Falck, Hans S.
  Social work: the membership perspective / Hans S. Falck; foreword by Thomas Owen Carlton.
      p. cm.—(Springer series on social work; v. 14)
   Bibliography: p.
   Includes index.
   ISBN 0-8261-4950-2
   1. Social service. I. Title. II. Series.
HV40.F2325 1988   88-9637
361.3—dc19   CIP

Printed in the United States of America

For my wife, Renate,
For my daughters,
Debbie, Ellen, and Sarah,
and
For the Six Million

Contents

Foreword

Every now and then, someone comes along who challenges fundamentally the ways in which social workers think about themselves, their clients, and the work they do. This does not happen very often. Robinson (1930) did it when she challenged social workers to incorporate personality theory into their knowledge base and to redefine relationship as the central core of their practice. Taft (1937) did it when she introduced the notions of agency function and process into social work thinking. Perlman (1957) influenced social work in lasting ways by integrating scientifically based problem solving and social work method. These theorists, and a few others, developed practice frameworks that influenced the thinking and activity of others for decades. Now, Falck has done it with his membership perspective of social work.

Thus, with the publication of this book, Falck takes his place among the handful of social workers whose formulations of practice are so significant that subsequent thought refers back to or derives from them. It is important, however, to recognize that his work differs from that of his predecessors in very basic ways, for Falck challenges the very foundation upon which all previous social work theory rests.

Over the years, social work theorists have struggled to reconcile the opposite ends of their client continuum (individual and community).

A result of their efforts is social work's much vaunted "dual focus." Although conceptualized by different writers in different ways and in various terms, the dual focus essentially casts one professional eye on clients who need personal help for personal problems, and the other on organizations, communities, policies, and programs. Falck challenges the dual focus in social work by demonstrating that its primary building blocks (the individual and the environment) are indefensible on scientific grounds, and thus cannot serve as the basis for a viable theory of social work practice.

Falck's membership perspective of social work is not a new effort to reconcile old variables. Rather, it is a revolutionary new approach to the whole field. Casual readers of this book who conclude that the issues that the membership perspective addresses are issues of semantics, therefore, will do themselves a great disservice. The membership perspective does not simply involve substituting certain words and phrases for others. It is a whole new way of thinking about people and working with them at all levels within the framework of social work purpose.

The central concepts of *member* and *membership* in Falck's perspective derive from an understanding of human beings and the ways they behave. This understanding differs from that found in other social work theories in that it rests on empirical findings from the biological and social sciences. These findings indicate that all human life and activity are group-based, that each human being is inextricably bound to others in permanent ways and cannot be removed or separated from them, not even for social work purposes. The perspective that derives from these facts is componential in nature; it is not a parts–whole perspective.

In applying the membership perspective of human behavior to social work, Falck accomplishes several important things and lays a number of old social work dichotomies to rest. For example, he shows that the longstanding "social versus psychological" argument is a tempest in a teapot, for the human being is *simultaneously* social and psychological; neither can be considered apart from the other. Falck also settles the historic "art versus science" debate in social work. He demonstrates that social work is both art and science because the understanding of human beings that underpins social work in the membership perspective embodies both empirically observable behavior and inferences drawn from that behavior.

Perhaps the most far reaching aspect of Falck's membership perspective is its dismissal of the "individual versus community" battle in social work thought, for once the dual focus is discarded, the issue itself ceases to exist. By viewing human activity in membership terms, the following things become evident: The question is not one of individual versus community; larger social configurations are membership groups too, and not environments; and the same principles and concepts apply to all of social work. This, the reader will discover, is true regardless of the size of the configuration of people being dealt with or the reason for engaging with them. Falck's notion of the social work helping group, of the client(s) and social worker as members of a common undertaking, applies to all. Falck thus unifies all of the profession's practice in a single framework.

When Robinson published her book in 1930, she let loose a psychoanalytic whirlwind throughout social work, the effects of which are still felt in social work practice to this day. Her work was based on her solid commitment to an untested (and to a large extent untestable) theory, but is has influenced social workers for decades, often without their even knowing it. In contrast, Falck has formulated an understanding of human life and social work practice that rests on hard scientific findings to a degree seldom thought of in social work and challenges social workers to reorient their profession in a new direction.

THOMAS O. CARLTON, D.S.W.
Professor, School of Social Work,
Virginia Commonwealth University
Richmond, Virginia

REFERENCES

Perlman, H.H. (1957). *Social casework: A problem-solving process.* Chicago: University of Chicago Press.

Robinson, V.P. (1930). *A changing psychology for social case work.* Chapel Hill: University of North Carolina Press.

Taft, J. (1937). The relation of function to process in social case work. *Journal of Social Work Process, 1*(1), 1–18.

Introduction

This book delineates the membership perspective of social work. The principles that guided its development are these:

1. Social work is a profession with its own central and identifiable characteristics.
2. Social work's common themes and principles articulate all social work practice, including diverse activities ranging from clinical social work to community social work.
3. The definition of specialized social work practice rests on the common principles that characterize the profession as a whole.

The argument set forth in this book is that the ability to think abstractly and to act concretely, often simultaneously, distinguishes the professional social worker from the nonprofessional. To view social work in membership management terms and to demonstrate practice consistent with this is the general aim of this book.

Throughout the book, recognition is given to the fact that social work has always been rather unusual in the breadth and depth of its orientation to human need. From its beginnings, social work has focused its attention on two major streams of thought and effort. One has emphasized social reform and includes advocacy and critique in terms of social justice, the distribution of resources, and community and neighborhood well-being; in short, the common and collective good. The second stream has emphasized personal functioning and group membership, and individual and family adjustment. The core consideration in this stream has been the personal needs of individuals.

More recently, social work theorists and practitioners have worked to achieve a convergence of these two streams. In the effort to promote this convergence, social workers have made substantive use of systems and ecological and environmental theories to develop more comprehensive approaches to social work practice (Briar, 1987; Germain & Gitterman, 1980; Meyer, 1970, 1984, 1987). While these efforts have undoubtedly helped to bring the concepts of the individual and the environment closer together, serious problems have also arisen. Among these problems is the inability to operationalize such terms as "environment," "ecology," "system," and "ecosystem" in terms that are meaningful and helpful in actual social work practice (Meyer, 1987). This inability, in turn, has produced numerous and often conflicting definitions of the same terms. The result is a violation of one of the basic rules of theory building: the criterion of internal consistency, which requires that concepts reflect semantic clarity and consistency in definition and use (Fawcett & Downs, 1986).

Meyer's (1987) overview of direct social work practice supports this conclusion. Meyer states that social workers face a bewildering variety of choices when it comes to selecting conceptualizations of practice and that there is "no empirical evidence that one or another approach is necessarily more effective than others" (p. 414).

For the development of the membership perspective, all of this has meant that theories and models based on the person-in-situation or other individualistic approaches that incorporate such concepts as environment, ecology, or system have been of limited use. These approaches are based on very different assumptions and knowledge about human beings from those that undergird the membership perspective. Indeed, the membership perspective reflects the rapidly growing ability of scientists in many fields to replace linear methods of reasoning with truly holistic models. These, in turn, call for a major rethinking of ideas that in social work have been largely considered to be settled. Meyer (1987), for example, asserts that whatever unifying perspectives may eventually emerge, they will "have to reflect the person-in-environment focus that has become central to the purpose of social work practice" (p. 414). An alternative to Meyer's conclusion, however, is to reexamine the person-in-environment paradigm and, assuming that more is desired than just a better fit between the concepts of person and environment, to abolish it on the basis of current knowledge of human behavior.

It is for this reason that the decision was made to review the major theories and models developed since 1940 that in one way or another conceptualize persons as individuals who, along with environments, are defined as objects of social work intervention. The results of this review are contained in Chapter 1 of this book. Ultimately, the reexaminaton led to questions about the ways clients are conceptualized by social workers in these various theoretical approaches and in daily practice.

Beyond the need to understand how social work theories have traditionally conceptualized human beings and clients, however, there is the additional need to explicate what social workers do. The position taken here is that this need is best met when the social worker action, or behavior, and social work frames of reference meet on common ground. Such meetings result in the ability of well-trained, experienced professionals to identify their techniques in terms of their theoretical allegiances and to modify the one or the other as knowledge demands. Questions about how clients are understood and how the core characteristics of social work are defined are, therefore, interdependent.

What these questions and this reexamination make clear is that despite the fact that forerunners of the membership perspective can be found throughout the history of social work, it is substantially different from all other approaches. Carlton (1984) meticulously documents sources in his application of the membership perspective to health social work. He is equally careful in his use of terminology, and his work demonstrates that membership terms have few, if any, antecedents in earlier approaches. In the membership perspective, no member is portrayed as an individual and no individual is portrayed as a member. Because of the regularity with which these two terms are employed interchangeably in social work theories and ultimately because language with its implications makes a difference, the use of major terms received a great deal of specific attention in the development of this book. This also explains why the number of references to other social work theories decreases as the membership perspective unfolds in the various chapters of this book. The point is that the membership perspective plows new ground.

It is difficult to change one's ways of thinking and expression when one is reared in the language of individualism. This is because individualism offers a flattering way of understanding oneself and others. The term *individual* stands not only alone in communicating meanings about specific people but, as all language does, it also affects human action when it is linked to other work. Thus, in the major social work theoretical frameworks, the term *individual* is combined with collectives that individualists refer to as *group, family, organization, environment*. Collectives, however, imply constituent individuals.

We can say in anticipation of the central ideas to be made explicit in this book that the concept of *member* stands halfway between the individual and the collectivity. The individual is recognizable by the attributes of uniqueness, separateness from others, even sacredness. Collectivity associates with group, community, ecology, and environment. Yet in both instances the constitutive, reductive element is the single person alone or in specifiable numbers.

The term *member* implies other members. The boundaries of the member are such that they make room for others in each and every instance. One does not need to advocate or argue for interrelatedness; it is there to begin with and only needs to be recognized as such. As we shall see, membership captures elements far more universal and more subtle than we are ready to say at this point of the argument.

The membership perspective rejects individualism and all of its concepts. Thus, understanding and absorbing the membership vocabularly and its view of the human condition requires major changes in thought and habit. The justification for these changes, indeed the most convincing argument for seriously challenging the validity of the individualistic language that has become ingrown in social work, is that science has changed the profession's ever expanding knowledge base and demands that its conceptual frameworks change as well.

This conclusion requires further elaboration. Cohen (1985) notes Freud's "special interest in the blows to man's self-image" stemming from the discoveries of Copernicus and Darwin. Copernicus, for example, demonstrated that man on his earth is but a speck in an unending universe and not even close to controlling himself in any major way. Copernicus, according to Freud, dethroned man from his fixed, central place in the universe. The biological blow was delivered by Darwin's theory of descent, which delineated "man's close kinship to other animals." Freud, in turn, showed how the relation of the conscious ego to an overpowering unconscious dealt a severe blow to human self-love. Thus, says Cohen, "Freud believed man had received staggering blows to his narcissistic self-esteem" in terms of cosmology, evolutionary biology, and psychology (pp. 360–361).

Viewed within the context of the history of science, the membership perspective's rejection of the narcissistic, ideological preoccupation with individual sovereignty takes the argument one step further. The membership perspective of life in general, and of social work in particular, must be understood, therefore, in terms of the sweep in all branches of science that ties the human being to nature as a componential element of infinity. As a component of infinity, the member is challenged to manage his or her personal autonomy as a self-conscious actor in the defense of self and other interests. The membership of all with all is the quantitative basis for human existence, while the qualities of membership styles and behavior are indeed subject to human consideration, choice, and modification.

This book is divided into nine chapters. The first chapter reviews major social work theories and approaches developed since 1940 and poses the essential problems inherent in individualism, upon which these developments rest. This chapter, therefore, serves as a backdrop for the explication of the membership perspective in the chapters that follow.

Chapter 2 explores the membership perspective of human behavior. It identifies knowledge sources that lead to the two principles that define membership in human life in general, which are, therefore, applicable to all social work thought and practice.

The third chapter applies the membership paradigm to professional social work practice. Not only is a new conceptualization of social work delineated, but each major term is defined. Chapter 3 also introduces the notion of the social work helping group as the means through which all social work intervention takes place.

Chapter 4 defines the social work client as member and explores the principles, nature, roles, requirements, and skills required by clientship. Chapter 5 similarly defines the social worker as member and delineates the components of social work activity.

Chapters 6 and 7 consider the social worker and the client together in terms of their common membership in the helping group. In these chapters, the content and styles, including techniques of social work intervention and assessment, are considered.

The eighth chapter is devoted to community social work from the perspective of membership. In demonstrating the applicability of all of the components of the membership perspective to community social work, the two historic streams of social work thought and effort (the common and collective good and personal functioning and group membership) are brought together in one, holistic conceptual framework for all of social work.

The final chapter consists of a summary discussion of the sense of community inherent in membership. This discussion focuses on the universality of membership as the irreducible variable in human life and on its reciprocal characteristics.

Practice vignettes and other examples of social work practice illustrate major points in each chapter. These examples are drawn from a wide range of social work settings and specializations. If some settings or specializations seem to receive more attention than others in the chapters that follow, this should not be taken to imply that the membership perspective favors some social work activities over others. All are simply illustrative. Indeed, if the chapters of this book make a single point, it is that there are universal common themes in social work that the membership perspective captures. These, in turn, lead to the formulation of those central statements and the articulation of those common characteristics that make all social work one profession.

In writing this book we resisted the constant seduction of engaging in social philosophy, which would have tied discussion of the membership perspective into the long history of analysis of the individual and the community. The reason for this resistance is that while social aspects of membership are given a prominent place in the argument to follow, it is not the only or even its most important attribute. The problem is magnified by the fact that in everyday parlance the terms *member* and *membership* are social science words.

At the same time that we include a social science definition of the member, there are other aspects which are biological, psychological, and symbolic in nature. Finally, we do not claim that the membership perspective contributes very much to social philosophy. It has a tone rather different from the one found in, for example, Bellah, Madsen, Sullivan, Swidler, and Tipton's recent book *Habits of the Heart* (1985). The latter is one more manifestation of the intense interest in individualism, which, of course, reaches back over many centuries beyond the term itself, for which credit is usually given to de Tocqueville. A volume on the history and ethics of the membership perspective, forcing a more contextual discussion than is possible in this book, will have to wait. In the meantime it seemed best to present the perspective in rather lean and uncluttered terms and leave its elaboration as well as tying it into the history of social thought for the future.

Special attention is to be placed on the biological component of membership, without which the entire perspective would be very different from what it, in fact, is. The research on this component alone is so extensive that we could touch upon it only to the degree that was necessary but without doing justice to its powerful suggestiveness in our increasing understanding of human life. It undermines, as it should, the inaccurate perception that social work is an applied social science and instead suggests that many of the principles that define everything from cell biology to the central nervous system, with particular emphasis on the behavior of the neurotransmitters, are applicable as well to other aspects of human life (P.M. Churchland, 1984; P.S. Churchland, 1986). This, too, is nearly unexplored in the social work literature, with the exception of the work of Johnson (1984).

Finally, it is easy to read the membership perspective as a rejection of individualism as ideology and the substitution of membership, as it were, as an ideological substitute. This is not the intent, nor does the argument rest on ideological grounds. Whereas there is hardly much scientific work that does not at some point embrace an ideological point of view, whether implicit or explicit or both, it does make a difference where the emphasis lies. In our case it is to be placed, as nearly as the material permits, on the scientific and factual as we have tried to demonstrate throughout this volume. If there appear to be value preferences at work, so much the better, since any helping profession needs to assess and examine its preferred beliefs. However, our primary intent is to present a view of the human condition and social work practice that is defensible, albeit unevenly so, on scientific grounds.

REFERENCES

Bellah, R.N., Madsen, R., Sullivan, W.M., Swidler, A., & Tipton, S.M. (1985). *Habits of the heart: Individualism and commitment in American life.* New York: Harper & Row.

Briar, S. (1987). Direct practice: Trends and issues. *Encyclopedia of social work* (18th ed.) (Vol. I, pp. 394–395). Silver Spring, MD: National Association of Social Workers.

Carlton, T.O. (1984). *Clinical social work in health settings: A guide to professional practice with exemplars.* New York: Springer Publishing Company.

Churchland, P.M. (1984). *Matter and consciousness.* Cambridge, MA: The MIT Press.

Churchland, P.S. (1986). *Neurophilosophy—Toward a unified science of the mind/brain.* Cambridge, MA: The MIT Press.

Cohen, J.B. (1985). *Revolution in science.* Cambridge: Harvard University Press.

Fawcett, J., & Downes, F.S. (1986). *The relationship of theory and research.* Norwalk, CT: Appleton-Century-Crofts.

Germain, C.B., & Gitterman, A. (1980). *The life model of social work practice.* New York: Columbia University Press.

Johnson, H.C. (1984). The biological bases of psychopathology. In F.J. Turner (Ed.), *Adult psychopathology, a social work perspective* (pp. 6–72). New York: The Free Press.

Meyer, C.H. (1970). *Social work practice—A response to the urban crisis* (pp. 147–185). New York: The Free Press.

Meyer, C.H. (1984). Selecting appropriate practice models. In A. Rosenblatt & D. Waldfogel (Eds.), *Handbook of clinical social work* (pp. 736–737). San Francisco: Jossey-Bass.

Meyer, C.H. (1987). Direct practice in social work: Overview. *Encyclopedia of social work* (18th ed.) (Vol. I, pp. 409–422). Silver Spring, MD: National Association of Social Workers.

Acknowledgments

For anyone who entered the social work profession in the 1950s, the last 35 years have been full of excitement and some disappointment. The excitement comes from being a member of a profession that has reached a state of development, indeed maturity, that borders on the spectacular. The disappointment derives from the continuing difficulties American society creates for itself by its ambivalence over its own needs for civilized and decent health and social welfare systems. On the whole, however, the disappointments have been outweighed by the advances of social work, advances to which many have contributed.

The teachers who influenced the writing of this book are many. Some stand out in my mind for their contributions to its evolution over time. I remember with gratitude my teacher Paul K. Weinandy, who demonstrated to his students what membership means. He taught me more about what social work could be than anyone I can remember. The 35 years that have passed since I first walked into his social agency have not dimmed either the memory or the validity of what he taught.

The late Talcott Parsons was the source of my interest in linking sociology and psychoanalytic object-relations theory. It was his work on social structure and the development of personality that pointed out to me Freud's contribution to the integration of sociology and psychology. I well remember my excitement upon first reading Parsons' work and the subsequent promise I made to myself that my contribution, if any, would be to further investigate this idea. This book is the result of that promise.

Emanuel Tropp pushed my thinking forward. His careful scholarship has been of benefit to the whole profession. In this connection, thanks must also go to the late William Schwartz. Widely misunderstood and somewhat misread to this day, Schwartz's influence remains a powerful motivation for me and for many others to continue to push forward. Even when Bill and I disagreed, it was always with mutual respect and, on my part, with admiration for his scholarship and his skill in self-expression.

I can hardly say enough about the opportunities for study and research I have had at the Virginia Commonwealth University School of Social Work. Elaine Z. Rothenberg, former Dean of the School of Social Work, who brought me to Richmond, and Grace E. Harris, her successor, deserve my thanks for creating an atmosphere in which serious scholarship over extended periods of time has been possible. I give that thanks gladly.

Bryant Mangum, of Virginia Commonwealth University's Department of English, also deserves my gratitude. He agreed to edit the manuscript, no mean task for someone not used to my Germanicisms.

In the School of Social work, my closest collaborators over the years of my tenure have been Thomas O. Carlton and Dennis L. Poole. Both are first-rate scholars and do honor to anyone fortunate enough to be able to work with them. They read and critiqued the manuscript in detail and their contributions are beyond counting. Poole asked all the right questions. Carlton contributed his enormous knowledge and skill, and also his memory of what I have written over the last 25 years. My gratitude to him is to be found in whatever contribution this book might make to social work thought and practice. He has had a major share in its development.

The contributions my wife, Renate Forssmann-Falck, M.D., made go far beyond what it is customary for spouses to be thankful for. She is a fine scholar in her own right. I have benefited from her training in internal medicine and in psychiatry, which has heavily influenced my thinking. She also encouraged me to undertake the vicissitudes of learning the fundamentals of neuroscience in the classroom, laboratory, and dissection room. Her contributions to this work extend through all of it. Sally Companion provided invaluable assistance in typing and editing various versions of the manuscript. I thank her.

Finally, all those students and colleagues who are less concerned with their entitlements than with the needs of their clients and their own abilities to help them continue to teach me and to give me confidence in the profession's future. I thank them.

HANS S. FALCK, Ph.D., F.R.S.H.
Richmond, Virginia

The Case of the Split Social Work World: Basic Concepts in Social Work Theories

1

Social work has divided the attributes of people into three parts: the biological, the psychological, and the social; and by relinking them to each other, it has tried to resolve the split (i.e., the biopsychosocial). The main reason for this split is the profession's weddedness to individualism. Because the individual is an insufficient conceptualization of the human situation, at least for social work purposes, and also on scientific grounds, the profession developed the so-called dual model of social work practice (i.e., individual and environment).

Since social work is a practice profession, it defines and refines its knowledge about people in practical, usable terms. The question is not what is the state of mankind, but how such configurations of people as individuals, groups, organizations, and society are to be understood. All definitions must pass the test of usefulness; and if this means a certain amount of distortion as one moves from basic science to applications in practice, it is a price to be paid.

In reviewing social work literature, the theorist is faced with problems that apply to no other profession. These problems have to do with the fact that social work has been subject to attack from within and without the profession for a great many years, and that these sallies against it have been damaging to the profession. At times, the internal condemnations have been both radical in content and

1

in method. Fischer (1976), for example, claimed that without commitment to evaluative research, the self-corrective functions of scientific work, and a stronger empirical base than had been the case, "there would indeed appear to be little justification for the continued existence of the institution of social casework" (p. 145). Government officials and others have been unhappy with social work for political and ideological reasons, as the profession itself understands well enough (Stewart, 1985).

The critique of the dual focus in social work (individual and environment) in the remaining chapters of this book utilizes the insights and the achievements of colleagues and teachers, current and past, and thus follows the century-long efforts of countless others. It is they who laid the foundation that informs all new social work models, perspectives, and insights. The membership perspective presented in this book, therefore, represents continuity, despite its insistence that it is time to rethink fundamentals.

The position taken here is that growth and development in professions are the result of consistent review, research, and political processes. The method must be critique, not criticism; the intent must be to help social work grow and flourish, not to destroy hard-won gains. At the same time, agreement with social work's individualism and its distortions of the human condition is avoided. But before individualism and the dual focus in social work that stems from it can be rejected, the task is to show how individualism has manifested itself as the central guiding concept in social work thought and practice.

HOW SOCIAL WORK VIEWS
THE HUMAN CONDITION

Social work literature describes the human situation as consisting of the biological, the psychological, and the social. Since practically no attention is actually rendered to the physical existence of people in social work education and practice, it has received only marginal attention in social work theory. Hence, the focus in social work historically has been on the psychological and the social, and perceived in individual terms.

The Individual

The term *individual* stands for the biological and the psychological attributes of persons. Most social workers see the individual as the most basic of human units.

Historically, the aims of social work have been such that the term *individual* came to define self-realization, self-determination, self-fulfillment, and access to power and resources. Therefore, the individual became the unit of service in social casework.

Beyond the rather obvious attributes of the term, *individual* is associated with boundedness—that is, a clear circumference in the physical sense (Van der Veelde, 1985) and psychological sense. Here one speaks of identity and of ego boundary. In addition, the idea of oneness is linked to uniqueness in order to attain the image of differentness and distinctiveness from others. Other implied attributes of the individual are specialness ("there is only one like you"), centrality, self-containment, and self-sufficiency.

A term with as many subtle meanings as "individual" offers both flexibility and imprecision. Because everyone knows the meaning of the term, no one defines it; because no one defines it, it is used with near abandon; and an aura of self-evidentness undermines accountability for its use. "Individual" may seem satisfactory for daily use; it is inadequate for scientific endeavor.

The Group

The word *group* has met with difficulties of definition, both in the social sciences and in social work literature. In one sense, it is defined by size (i.e., the "small group" or such large units as legislative committees or assemblies). In a second sense, group is linked to collectivity. In still another sense, group is tied to the term *social,* thereby contrasting the group with individuals. Yet all writers suggest that groups, organizations, and collectivities consist of individuals.

Although the group is the apparent unit of service in most theories of social work with groups, the actual unit of service is most often the individual, inasmuch as the group is the means to individual change (Glasser, Sarri, & Vinter, 1974; Shulman, 1984). In social work theory the group is seldom the end of social work practice.

To most people, including social workers, *society* is incomprehensible, other than in symbolic terms. As is the case with the individual, the term *society* is so broad that it allows for nearly any form of characterization. In order to bring it into a usable state, social workers often conceptualize society as if it were a person (i.e., society believes, thinks, acts, and regards or disregards). When treated as if it were a person, society is subject to praise for its good intentions and to criticism for its inconsistent and discriminatory performance, depending on one's perceptions.

The most general of group terms in social work language is the so-called *social environment*. The social environment includes every human phenomenon outside of the individual. Thus, all schools of social work offer courses in "human behavior and the social environment," and social work theorists define various kinds of environments (Germain, 1980; Germain & Gitterman, 1980; Schwartz, 1961, 1976). The point is that the so-called environment is rarely defined as consisting of people subject to the same characteristics as social work clients. If the concept is to be of use in social work, however, environment cannot be an "it." To be useful, environment must be something more than an enveloping phenomenon leaving the individual surrounded, so to speak, while standing at the center. To dichotomize the human condition as the individual and the environment, even if the latter is social, reduces serious consideration about the nature of society to the impossible.

HOW SOCIAL WORK CONCEPTUALIZES CLIENTS

Social work's conceptualizations of clients can be documented by focusing on individuals and groups as they appear in the literature. Although examples of definitions of individuals and groups exist reaching back to the early part of the century (Richmond, 1917), the review that follows focuses on representative literature published since 1940, a span of time that can somewhat arbitrarily be called the modern period.

In general, social work during the last 100 years has defined, combined, and recombined its interests in the individual, group, and society in different ways. Bloom (1983) recounts the history of these efforts in his attempt to portray those variables that the profession's researchers utilize in evaluative studies of social work practice. Bloom's review, in particular, illustrates what it is that the profession considers worthy of evaluation and, therefore, the ways it conceives the objects of social work intervention, that is, the individual and the small group. The object of intervention becomes, therefore, the object of evaluation. Thus, the question is not so much what it is that the social worker did, but what it is that occurred in the lives of the clients as a result of the work. Once it is clear how social workers describe their clients, who and what it is the researcher/practitioner evaluates also becomes clear.

Weick (1984) addresses the same problem, but in a rather different way. She asks whose responsibility one's illness is. After discussing the question in social context terms, she concludes that illness is the responsibility of the individual. But she also suggests that the idea of individualism needs redefinition in order that the profession be able to capitalize upon its advantages more than it has done in the past. According to Weick, the self-responsibility movement in health care reinforces social work's traditional view of individualism and too often results in blaming the victim:

> Social work has adhered to a belief in the capacity of both individuals and collections of individuals to transform themselves. Even though the radical nature of this belief has not been expressed with the complexity and depth it deserves, there has been an admirable professional allegiance to this view of human potential. (p. 24)

Weick concludes that healing is a metaphor that is holistic in outlook. She proposes that individual self-regulation attends to both itself and the social context and portrays the optimism needed to go into a future marked by self-creation (p. 23).

In discussing the use of network concepts in social work theory and practice, Ell (1984) states that "enhancing the goodness-of-fit between individuals and their personal networks as well as providing professional support are routine goals of social work practice" (p. 141). Ell does not view individuals and their personal networks as one unit, since she uses the connective "and" to split them.

Chatterjee (1984) is one of the rare current writers who has recognized the ideological implications of a profession wed to individualism. "American culture and the social work profession are ideological subscribers to individualism and the equality of individuals. . . . [P]rofessional socialization in social work education reinforces the above ideological preference" (p. 77).

In their consideration of the individual as the historically preferred focus in social work thought and practice, three documents illustrate Chatterjee's point forcefully. The first is "The Social Worker's Creed," by Linton Swift (1946). The second and third are the codes of ethics published by the National Association of Social Workers in 1977 and 1983.

Swift (1946) wrote:

> I respect the dignity of the individual human personality as a basis of all human relationship. . . . I shall base my relations with others on their qualities as individual human beings. . . . I believe that an individual's greatest pride, as well as his greatest contribution to society may lie in the ways in which he is different from me and from others, rather than in the ways in which he conforms to the crowd. I shall therefore accept these differences and endeavor to build a useful relationship upon them. (p. 1)

In 1977, the Delegate Assembly of the National Association of Social Workers adopted a Code of Ethics that mandated belief in individualism implicitly, as well as explicitly. The Code, for example, stated the following:

> I regard as my primary obligation the welfare of the individual or the group served, which includes action for improving social conditions. (NASW, 1977, p. 1067)

In 1980, the National Association of Social Workers adopted a new Code of Ethics. While this version eliminated the sentence cited above, it nevertheless employs the term *individual* throughout. The overall impression is that the Association gave little or no attention to the scientific standing of the term and, in all probability, takes it for granted.

Reamer (1983), who is known for his work on social work ethics, also uses language that perpetuates the separation of individual and environment, but he does see them in some correlational stance to each other. He points out that although social workers are "predisposed to identify and understand both individual and environmental determinants of clients' problems," it is evident that social workers differ in the extent to which they would say that clients are responsible for their own difficulties (p. 633).

In a discussion of bias in research on social work effectiveness, Kagle and Cowger (1984) point to the danger of "blaming the client" for his or her difficulties. They note that in much of the research the changes that individuals make, or fail to make, are evaluated while the role of the environment, the social structure, is overlooked (pp. 347–351). They document their claims through a review of recent evaluation studies. In doing so, they document the intellectual biases in social work research conceptualization and emphasis which, they note, too often ignore environmental deficits in the social and political structures of society while they give credit to or place blame upon the relatively helpless individual. They conclude, "Despite the profession's avowed commitment to person-in-situation definitions, the social work practice literature contains many examples of blaming the client" (p. 347). It should be noted, however, that Kagle and Cowger do not question the basic formulation: the person-in-situation. To them, as for virtually all authors except Carlton (1984, 1986), individuals and situations (environments) remain unquestioned.

Coulton (1981) summed up the current conceptual map of social work as follows:

> . . . substantial agreement seems to exist among social workers that the focus of social work is the person and the environment in interaction and that the profession's purpose is to promote or restore a mutually beneficient interaction between individuals and society. This consensus can be seen in the earlier special issue of *Social Work,* devoted to conceptual frameworks as well as in other writings by various leaders in the field (p. 26).

Coulton uses the terms *person* and *individual* interchangeably. She is explicit in distinguishing between the individual and the environment and by commenting upon the fit between them. However, no attempt is made to integrate or synthesize them.

Having suggested the broad outline of the discussion to follow, our attention now turns to selected social work theories that offer, or claim to offer, basic conceptualizations from which many others have derived their ideas. They span the entire modern period.

MAIN CURRENTS IN SOCIAL WORK THEORY SINCE 1940

The Theory and Practice of Social Case Work by Gordon Hamilton first appeared in 1940. The influence of this book was of the greatest significance to the many social workers who came into the field during and after the Second World War. It was written during the Great Depression and appeared subsequent to the outbreak of the war in Europe. But the United States did not go to war until late in 1941, and in America the economic crisis was still in the air when Hamilton's book was published. To teach and practice social work from an individualistic, psychoanalytical standpoint alone, therefore, would have meant being blind to the realities of the era. Hamilton is explicit about the need for a dual emphasis, the individual and the environment, as the basis of social casework practice:

> Central to any discussion is the understanding that problems are both individual and social, that a case is always a complex of inner and outer factors. We know that there are unmanageable factors in the environment and that no case work approach will make them "more manageable." (p. 25)

In a more subtle and genuine way, Hamilton elaborates on the individual–environment link:

> The concept of the "family as the unit of work" meant to the early case worker, doing services for all the family from parents to baby. Relief, helping papa to a job, mama to a budget, teeth for grandpa, camp for Johnny, tonsils out for Marie, clothing for everyone was the pattern. This was in part because the family worker was usually called in by the breakdown of the bread-winner through illness or unemployment. (p. 236)

Here, Hamilton clearly writes of an earlier time in social work, but it was also true in her own generation when large numbers of social workers confronted severe economic dislocation on a daily basis. It would have been unusual indeed had a scholar of Hamilton's stature written other than she did. The knowledge available at the time could not have led to the conclusion that the individual–environment split is unnecessary and that its elimination allows clients and social workers to do their mutual work quite differently than was the case in her time.

In a series of three articles published in 1949, Bowers identified 34 definitions of social casework available in the literature up to that time. Among these, nine designate the individual as the subject and object of social work; seven more add to or qualify the individual in terms such as *relationship, activity, conduct, needs.* Bowers also offers a definition of his own at the end of the third article. More than 35 years later, the reader can identify in Bower's definition all of the elements currently popular in the ecological model and other formulations of the 1980s:

> Social casework is an art in which knowledge of human relations and skill in relationship are used to mobilize capacities in the individual and in resources in the community appropriate for better adjustment between the client and all or any part of his total environment. (Bowers, 1949, p. 417)

In 1958, Werner Boehm offered the following definition of social work:

> Social work seeks to enhance the social functioning of individuals, singly and in groups, by activities focused on their relationships which constitute the interaction between man and his environment. These activities can be grouped into three functions: restoration of impaired capacity, provision of individual and social resources, and prevention of social dysfunction. (p. 18)

Many of Hamilton's contemporaries espoused essentially the same basic concepts. Basing their theoretical orientation in Freudian psychology, they were known collectively as the Diagnostic School of Social Work. Primary among Hamilton's successors is Florence Hollis (1964), whose definition of social casework as psychosocial therapy maintained major focus on the individual. The third edition of her book, co-authored with Mary E. Woods (1981), attempts to broaden the focus of psychosocial therapy, but the major unit of attention remains the individual.

A second major school of thought in the development of social work theory during this period was known as the Functional School. Rooted in Rankian psychology, its primary theorists were Jessie Taft (1944), Virginia P. Robinson (1943), and Kenneth L.M. Pray (1949). Although functional theory emphasizes the process of helping the client in relation to agency function as a major theoretical principle, its attention is focused on the "individual difference" of each client. Primary among the successors of Taft, Robinson, and Pray was Ruth E. Smalley (1967), who, although her psychology of the individual continued to differ from that of Hamilton, nevertheless maintained the split between individual and group, as do the most recent proponents of the functional approach (Arnold & Bloom, 1981; Ryder, 1976).

In 1957, Helen H. Perlman published *Social Casework—A Problem Solving Process,* a book that still influences social work practice. The author offered the following definition of social casework: "Social casework is a process used by certain human welfare agencies to help individuals to cope more effectively with their problems in social functioning" (p. 4). Basing her formulations on ego psychological theory, Perlman was clearly aware of the "social" that is intrinsic in social casework. Hence, the perception of the human condition inherent in her definition of social casework is more balanced than others. Nevertheless, Perlman, too, emphasized the individual in her model. Indeed, it is the systematization of social casework in the scientific mode of problem solving, rather than her dealing with the individual and individualism, that is the most lasting contribution of her model.

Focus on the individual also influenced the development of group work theory. Coyle (1947, 1948) and Wilson and Ryland (1949), for example, carried the fundamental concepts that guided Hamilton's work into their own, as did H.U. Phillips (1957), although as a theorist of the Functional School her work was rooted in a different theory of psychology. Northen (1969) provides an apt illustration of the point. She opens her group work text with the statement that "[s]ocial work has as its primary concern the individual in his interpersonal relations and in his encounters with his environment" (p. 1).

Rarely, however, has the social work profession been influenced as profoundly and lastingly by a single article as it has been by William Schwartz's "The Social Worker in the Group" (1961). Schwartz believed that before one could or should define specialized methods in social work (in his case, social group work), a more comprehensive definition of the profession was needed. As Schwartz understood it, the social worker has to be viewed within the total context of the human situation. The social worker–client relationship is seen as reciprocal; and it is a one-to-one and a one-to-group relationship. At this point, Schwartz suggests that the client and the social worker are individuals who affect each other when so desired. He continues:

> We should suggest that the general assignment of the social work profession is to mediate the process through which the individual and his society reach out for each other through a mutual need for self-fulfillment. This presupposes a relationship between the individual and his nurturing group which we would describe as "symbiotic"— each needing the other for its own life and growth, and reaching out for the other with all the strength it can command at a given moment. (p. 15)

Schwartz (1976) is altogether clear that he aims at a holistic model. In fact, he specifies the conditions under which such a model is attainable. He quotes Parsons to say that "the very definition of an organic whole is as one within which *the relations determine the properties of its parts*. . ." (p. 173). He then cites Frank to the effect that what is needed is a "field concept describing circular, reciprocal relations. . . through which the component members of the field participate in and thereby create the field as a whole. . ." (p. 175). These are clearly holistic concepts and are internally consistent, with the exception of the fact that Parsons speaks of parts instead of components. Yet Schwartz's intent remains clear even though its realization is hampered by the atomistic tendency in social work theory building of conceiving of the client as the individual.

The social worker's role in his model, for example, is found essentially in what Schwartz called the "mediating function," a phrase that has become famous in the profession. The formulation of the mediating function appears to stem from the conceptual limitations of the notion of the individual inherent in Schwartz's definition of the group. That is, he defines the group as a collection of individuals "who need each other in order to work on certain common tasks, in an agency that is hospitable to those tasks" (p. 185). An additional problem is that as a mediator, the social worker is placed in an asocial stance, even though relationships, whether of enmity or friendship, move people closer, not further apart. Thus, the notion that one can "stand between" individuals and groups is questionable.

Here, one senses the asocial, spatial gap that has opened in the development of social work theory, a development that is out of line with current research findings on human development. Thus, Schwartz's model incorporates the same difficulty that basically individualistic models always do: Individualism separates. Schwartz continued his work well into the 1970s (Schwartz, 1976; Schwartz & Zalba, 1971), and its influence continues in the present. Lawrence Shulman (1984), for example, has demonstrated the application of Schwartz's framework to social work practice as a whole. Among Shulman's other notable contributions was to show how the use of a particular frame of reference influences the interpretation of research data, a contribution whose significance has been ignored too long.

During the decade 1970–1979, two other significant social work books appeared that should also be noted. Their importance lies in the fact that they are collections of theoretical statements by major authors that codify the predominant models of social casework and social work with groups. One volume, edited by Turner in 1974 and revised in 1979 and 1985, carries the title *Social Work Treatment: Interlocking Theoretical Approaches.* The other, edited by Roberts and Northen, is *Theories of Social Work with Groups,* published in 1976.

Turner (1979) addresses the nature of theory in social work. He defines the uses and limits of theory and notes that the term has been used rather loosely in the profession. He contends that in the future theory and practice will bear more directly identifiable mutual relationships than is presently the case. Dame Eileen Younghusband, a distinguished British social work educator who wrote the preface to the Turner volume, makes the same point about the role of empiricism in social work practice theory (pp. xiii–xiv). However, neither Turner nor his contributors offer definitions of major terms, nor do they question individualism and other key concepts in their statements about social work "treatment." Krill (1979), in his chapter on existential social work, comes closest to a definition of individualism, yet it is so indirect that it cannot really be regarded as a definition (pp. 147–176).

Theories of Social Work with Groups, edited by Roberts and Northen (1976), presents a variety of models in group work theory in social work. As in the Turner volume, a number of authors (12) present their formulations according to an outline provided by the editors. The concluding chapter by Roberts and Northen addresses directly the role of the individual and the group:

> Although the authors reported a strong commitment to the integrity and worth of the individual, and to his right to self-determination, there was variation in the client system chosen as the focus of the worker's activities. Two of the approaches, the *task-centered* and the *organizational content,* define the client system as the individual; two others, the *mediating* and the *developmental,* see the group itself as the primary client. Interestingly, all the authors who define a single system as the client either exclude or do not discuss family groups as appropriate targets and focus most, if not all, of their discussion on formed groups. In contrast, three of the authors, Hartford, Northen, and Somers, focus on dual client systems, the individual and the group. These authors see individual and group goals as intertwined in all types of groups, but point out that one or the other system may be the primary focus for the worker in a particular situation. (p. 376)

All of the theorists who contributed to the Turner volume and the Roberts and Northen book hold two ideas in common: (1) individuals exist; and (2) individuals are sometimes the "targets" of helpful interventions by social workers. In a more general way, they convey the message that to account for whatever else primary focus on the individual and individualism omits, the social aspects of life must be added to the individual. The clear impression is left that individuals are something other than social units.

During the social revolution of the 1960s, social work was criticized for being "too tied to the establishment" and for being too psychologically oriented. It was accused of ignoring social problems and of blaming the victim for his or her difficulties. It is beyond the purview of this chapter to examine the social change dynamics of the 1960s. Nevertheless, the social work writings of the 1970s cannot be understood without attending to the 1960s. Suffice it to say that after the 1960s never again did a major social work theorist ignore the "social," the "environmental," or the "social context," while remaining loyal to the individualism that runs through the entire history of modern social work. Strean (1979), best known for his writings on psychoanalytic social work, writes of the environment as "interfering with people's psychosocial functioning" (p. 155). Toseland and Rivas (1984) state that "workers should attend to three focal areas when practicing with any kind of treatment or task group: (1) the individual group member, (2) the group as a whole, and (3) the environment in which the group functions" (p. v).

Meyer (1970), in an unequivocal statement about the problem inherent in splitting the human being into parts, observes that

> . . . the primary work of social work is individualizing. . . A primary characteristic of an individualizing process is to differentiate people. . . . We will know him [the person] as an individual only through understanding his very particular needs, feelings, desires, physical and mental characteristics and styles of life. (pp. 107–109)
>
> [T]he accepted traditional social casework view of the *person-in-situation* illustrates the problem of separation between social and psychological sciences. This concept requires the connectives *in* or *and,* because both the person and the (social) situation have different theoretical components and are actually measured by completely different yardsticks. The sciences of sociology and psychology are conceived on different levels of abstraction and point toward different levels of intervention, and the state of knowledge is such that to compress both kinds of knowledge into one would either psychologize society or sociologize personality. (p. 126)

Similarly, social systems theory, although it first came to the social work scene in the 1950s, was seized on as an organizing framework in an effort to bring under one hat all of the pieces of social work, that is, client, environment, social worker (Hearn, 1958; Stein, 1974).

Under the influence of systems theory, the possibilities of groups, whether family groups or formed groups, began to receive increased attention and to play increasingly prominent roles in social work thought. Pincus and Minahan (1973), for example, defined social work in terms of focus on "the linkages and interactions of people and resource systems and the problems to be faced in the functioning of both individuals and systems" (p. 9). Garvin and Seabury (1984) employ a systems approach to consider communities and organizations as elements of client environments. Compton and Galloway (1984) use systems theory to structure their generalist framework. Lonergan (1985), however, is more cautious in her use of systems theory, noting that it only represents a "beginning attempt to recognize, appreciate, and understand the whole" and that the implications of "all the systems" for "treatment interventions in individual and group therapy" have only been glimpsed (p. 7).

Carel B. Germain is one of the most prolific of social work's current theorists (Germain, 1976, 1978, 1979, 1980). Her approach to practice has been applied to the fields of child welfare (Germain, 1985), health (Germain, 1977, 1984; Schlesinger, 1985), genetics (Schild & Black, 1984), school social work (Winters & Easton, 1983), to social work with groups (Balgopal & Vassil, 1983), and to community social work (Germain, 1986).

Germain (1980) addresses the concept of ecology as social context and lists several types of environments: technological, informational, statutory and regulatory, economic and political, institutional, and cultural (pp. 483–485). Her approach, also known as the life model (Germain & Gitterman, 1980), emphasizes an ecological assessment of the social context, argues for holism, and defines the central dimensions for social work interventions as the transactions between people and their environments. However, Clemenger (1980) observes that a weakness of this approach is that it "purports to describe the life model as an integrated approach to social work practice that is, on the whole, individual–client oriented" (p. 122).

Why Germain conceptualized social work as concerned with the transactions of individuals and environments seems clear. Splitting the human condition into individuals and environments is the historical main current in social work theory building. Thus, Germain and Gitterman, as so many others before them, fell into the same logical splitting. Beginning with the premise that people are to be respected as individuals, regardless of any circumstances other than that they are human beings, the authors end up with a series of unexamined, nonempirically based statements about individuals and environments. When the individual and the environment are placed opposite each other, or when the individual is placed in the middle of an imaginary circle and all else is designated as the environment, the individual can indeed be understood as being overwhelmed, powerless, disenfranchised and, therefore, in need of social work help. Individuals come first and last. Thus, while the model maintains self-sufficiency as the main ingredient of the American Dream, the result is that the dream can also be a nightmare.

It is erroneous to conclude that by 1980 the social work profession had discovered that the individual and the group had to be taken into account simultaneously in social work thought and practice. The split was already present in 1940, and even earlier. One can say, however, that by 1980 the error had become codified. This codification stands at the end of a long process.

The fact that the dual focus in social work has lasted so long is a result of dissatisfaction with two shortcomings in social work theory and practice. One is the tendency of individualism to exclude adequate attention to social factors. The other shortcoming is less obvious. It has to do with the continued critique of Freudian-derived psychoanalytic approaches. Psychoanalysis is widely viewed as representing the epitome of individualism, both by its supporters and by its critics. However, this conclusion overlooks the fact that without social interaction there would be no way of understanding intrapsychic conflict. Interaction equals social behavior. One may value behavior more or less, or think of it as merely a means to get at what interests the psychoanalytically oriented social worker most, that is, the unconscious. Yet the fact remains that only behavior, verbal and nonverbal, brings the social worker and the client to an understanding of personality dynamics. Personality expresses itself in behavior, and psychoanalysis is, therefore, a social psychology. To classify psychoanalysis as altogether psychological in nature distorts it and does it a grave injustice. To do so also fails to take into account its enormous influence on American social life.

In summary, all of the authors cited above are sensitive to the fact that individuals cannot exist alone. All find some way of dealing with this truth, albeit in different ways. Essentially, their solutions attempt to counterbalance the preoccupation with the individual by linking the individual to the environment. This results in a dialectic aimed at evenhandedness and, more significantly, at accounting for a multiplicity of factors that influence society at large and clients in particular. Concisely stated, the dialectic takes on the language of individual and group, individual and society, individual (or person) and environment. What this dialectic fails to do is to portray a true holistic and multivariate model—one that avoids the split of individual and group.

THE NATURE OF THE SPLIT

In order to define the nature of the split in the social work world, it is useful to analyze five postulates about individuals that express the split:

1. *A human being's uniqueness entitles him or her to needed satisfactions.*

In this statement, others exist to meet individual needs to which one is entitled. It is a statement about reciprocal egoism. There is nothing in it that implies that the most destitute of recipients of social work help could have anything at all to give to others when, in fact, they might and often do.

2. *A human being's views of himself or herself suggest that the highest level of behavior is reflected in his or her independence.*

Similarly, this statement defines independence in individualistic terms and explains why self-determination shows up in social work as an allegedly democratically determined right. But this democracy is minimal because it assumes that self-determination speaks to independence, which is limited only by the extent to which others enjoy the same separate right. Implicit in social work's usual definition of the right to self-determination is a total disregard of the fact that all decisions, self-determined or not, are social in nature and are, therefore, of immediate interest to others.

3. *A human being's relationships to others are characterized by attributes of himself or herself alone; he or she is the actor of consequence.*

This statement addresses a related issue. It is that individualism describes relationships with others in one-way language. Consider the following case vignette, for example.

> The client said that she told her friend that she ought to drop her boyfriend because he was mistreating her. The friend replied that he was none of her business and that she should keep her nose out of it, otherwise she wouldn't talk to her about the matter anymore. The client said this upset her. The social worker told the client that it was altogether her decision whether she wanted to be intrusive enough to lose her friend or take the advice and stop invading her privacy.

In this example, the impression is left that all that counts is what the client does and what the social worker thinks about it. Whether the social worker's comments were clinically appropriate is not the matter of concern here. What is of concern is that the behavior of the client and her friend is viewed as one-way, rather than as reciprocal in nature. Had the social worker taken a reciprocal approach, he or she might well have focused on the mutual interactions that undoubtedly were part of the situation the client described. As it was, the client and the social worker both saw the client as the actor of consequence and the friend as someone else, "out there."

4. *A human being defines his or her identity by what distinguishes him or her from other people.*

This statement speaks to the issue of individual identity. In the individual/society split, the "I am I" and "you are you" implies that if one has a body of one's own, as do other persons, it means separation and thus confirms identity. An important modification of this occurs in the work of Margaret Mahler and her associates (1975), who hold that when a child attains a sense of separateness from his or her mother, this occurs within, rather than outside, the ongoing relationship of the two to each other. "Individuation" is the term Mahler and her associates use to describe becoming a self that is the product of and contributor to the ongoing relations people need to survive. The work of Mahler and her colleagues stands in major contrast to the implications of Statement #4, which suggest that there are fixed boundaries in nature between dependent and independent persons.

5. *A human being defines himself or herself as "free" by the degree to which he or she makes decisions leading to maximum benefit to himself or herself.*

This last statement postulates that freedom is an individual benefit that occurs without reference to others. What this assertion omits is that everyone has to live with his or her own decisions and their consequences. What is meant here is that each individual has to face the consequences of actions taken. Once again, the damage done by a misunderstanding of the concept of self-determination is evident.

To the degree that these five postulates are true, one can see at once why environment or some other context has to be added to the individual to obtain a sense of completion. Nevertheless, what unifies these five postulates is that they characterize the individual as a closed system. They create boundaries that are overdrawn and give the impression that in order to deal with others fruitfully, one must be a closed, bounded self first, rather than a person who contributes to others and is contributed to by others. Thus viewed, individual and group belong to two different worlds.

FOUR WAYS TO REPAIR THE SPLIT

The operative terms in the postulates listed and elaborated on above are separateness, independence, self-attribution, distinctiveness, and freedom. Each is attached to and elaborates upon the idea of the individual, indeed defines it. To deal with what each of these terms omits, social work theorists have used at least four alternative or remedial approaches.

Addition

The first alternative retains the basic idea, namely the individual as the irreducible unit of human life, but combines it with its counterpart, the group, for example, the individual *and* the group. This is the additive style of repairing the split, of taking into account whatever is outside the individual. This alternative is akin to Durkheim's definition of the term "social" as all of those "manners of acting, thinking, and feeling external to the individual, which are invested with a coercive power by virtue of which they exercise control over him" (Durkheim, 1982, p. 59). Durkheim, however, did not reduce the social to the personal or individual. The aim in the additive solution is to obtain a more complete picture of the human situation than the individual can provide when left to himself or herself.

Analysis of the way in which the social work theorists cited above dealt with the individual–collectivity problem shows that most can be classified into the category of addition. This is the approach taken by Bloom (individual, family, *and* large social system), Reamer (correlating individual *and* collectivity with relative emphasis on both), Coulton (aiming for mutually beneficial interaction between individuals and society), Hamilton (individual *and* environment), Coyle, Wilson and Ryland, and Phillips (individual *and* group), Pincus and Minahan (linkages and interactions of people *and* resource systems), Toseland and Rivas (individuals, groups, *and* environments), and the authors in the books edited by Turner and by Roberts and Northen (individuals *and* groups). Boehm (1959) employed the additive solution in his phrase "man and his environment."

While all of the above examples illustrate the additive mode of healing the split, it can be observed that few authors add the parts in the same way. The exceptions to this conclusion are the group work authors, Coyle, Wilson and Ryland, Phillips, Toseland and Rivas, and Roberts and Northen, all of whom use the "individual *and* the group" formulation.

Hyphenation

A second way to overcome the limitations of individualism is expressed by the use of hyphens. Here, too, the aim appears to be to obtain a fuller picture of people, but the means differ from the additive solution in that terms are hyphenated in a row-like, serial sense. The widely used "person-in-situation" illustrates this alternative. The objective is that no one term becomes subordinate to the other, other than indirectly as demonstrated by always placing the word "individual" first and the appended terms "in-the-situation" afterwards. No one, for example, has conceptualized the alternative as "situation-in-person." It should be observed, moreover, that the hyphen method overcomes, at least to a degree, the rigid boundaries implicit in the additive one, where each element, namely individual and group, undergoes no change. The hyphenation solution at least begins to work on this problem.

Ell (1984) takes a hyphenated approach in which there is some suggestion that the individual and collectivity elements have some inherent relationship. Ell does this by asserting that in working with clients, the social worker should look for a goodness-of-fit between them.

Mediation

The third solution is the mediation method of repairing the split. This method is best illustrated by Schwartz, as discussed above. Mediating is a bridging function that Schwartz assigns to the social worker in the group. The worker lends the clients a vision of what the group might achieve, and mediates between and among individuals, groups, and institutions. As noted, the mental image this creates is at least the possibility that the social worker can stand between social units without being a component of any of them. Schwartz, as much as anyone, tried to show how social work fits a general systems approach. The split he portrayed, however, was that of the individual and of society, both of which he saw as "reaching out for each other" with the assistance of the social worker, who, through mediation, linked them to each other. Schwartz did not agree that splitting the individual and society was his intent, but judging on the basis of language alone, one once again confronts the underlying constraint, namely the individual.

Parts–Whole

A fourth method of repairing the split is the parts–whole formulation implicit in most social work writing based on social systems theory and, for that matter, in much of the holistic literature in social work. The parts–whole approach has some similarities to the additive method in that it brings together pieces that by themselves are too incomplete for social work purposes. The parts–whole solution states that only integration, not just the addition of parts, will do. It holds, for example, that as any given part of a system changes, so do all the other parts of the system and the system itself. As one family member changes, for example, so do the others and the entire family, or group, or society. Several authors take the parts–whole approach. This is the impression left by Weick (1984), who conceptualizes a dynamic matrix of individual, society, and environment shaping individuals, and by Germain and Gitterman (1980), who assert the wholeness of individual and environment in an "ecological" model.

One would support this method of healing the split were it not for the implications of the term "parts." Parts in this connection usually mean individuals, as in "individuals are the constituent parts of groups." Again, careful examination shows that in systems theory, as in other formulations, the individual is the irreducible unit of analysis. Besides, parts may have an independent existence as well as play their roles within the whole. A car wheel can exist separately from the car, even if the basic intent in building it is to enable the car to move.

In conclusion, whether any of the authors cited above fit in any one of these categories (addition, hyphenation, mediation, parts–whole) is of little importance. Nor does it matter that several of the authors cited did not address the nature of the individual–collectivity relationship directly. What is important is that all, with the possible exception of Perlman, use language that clearly conceptualizes persons as individuals and that the corollary and/or alternative to the individual is the environment or some other-named collective. This is true of Kagle and Cowger (who do object to blaming the victim through the types of designs used in evaluation studies), Meyer (who strongly argues that the aim of social work should be individualization of clients), and of Turner and Bowers, neither of whom seems to address the subject in conceptual terms.

Undoubtedly, there are other ways of explaining further the various solutions to what has been referred to here as "the split." It should be clear from what has been said thus far, however, that existing formulas to deal simultaneously with the individual and the environment, however named, are without exception individualistic in nature.

SOME FURTHER CONSIDERATIONS

Implicit in the concepts social work uses to understand the human situation is a question about parts and wholes that deserves greater consideration than it has received. It is a question about the logical state of wholes and their elements. This matter will be considered more fully in the next chapter, which summarizes the membership perspective. The point that must be made here, however, is that the split between an individual and the group proceeds from the standpoint that the parts (individuals) account for the group (whole), so that the group becomes the superordinate concept. The reasoning is inductive. By attempting to create holistic concepts without changing the way in which social workers reason, the undertaking has lost most of its impact, for the truth is that the wholes precede parts. The result of the failure to understand holism, while attempting to build it into social work theory and thought, are the four modes that attempt to heal the split. This failure to understand holism has also protected the intellectual and ideological sanctity of individualism. The significance of this observation can be seen in the fact that for more than 45 years little has changed in social work conceptualizations of who the client is. It is as if the only change has been to confront the individual with the environment, without spelling out any really usable relationship between the two.

Even Gordon Hearn (1958), the most sophisticated of social work scholars in systems theory, holds that "Each system consists of objects which are simply the parts or components of the system; there are attributes which are the properties of the objects; and there are relationships among the objects and their attributes which tie the system together" (p. 39). What Hearn says is that each group consists of individuals who are the components of groups; there are attributes that describe individuals, and there are relationships among individuals that make groups. What is omitted is that the whole, the community or group, comes first; that the universe is not invented or created by individuals but is, in fact, irreducibly whole.

In modern times, the idea that one begins with parts (individuals) and reduces everything else to them is too easy an accommodation to a scientific method that cannot deal with wholes. As a reflection of human reality it was, and is, fundamentally faulty. D. C. Phillips describes this fundamental fault (1976) in his critique of General Systems Theory (GST):

> A second objection to the simple cure—selecting the entities that form a relevant system—is that the general systems theorist has not gone far enough. He also has to show that in isolating this system from the other entities with which it is normally interrelated he has not introduced artifacts, or as Beer put it, that he has not committed an "annihilating divisio." One of the main points made by GST is that the interrelationships between parts of a system are of vital importance. And in isolating a system for study the theorist is necessarily severing some interrelationships—the very thing his own creed tells him should not be done. (p. 63)

Phillips's critique of General Systems Theory raises the same essential question that social work's traditional method of reasoning also raises. Both have to do with the reducibility of social existence (group and community) to the psychological (individual). It is incumbent upon us to find other models that accommodate concepts that describe life not only sociologically and psychologically, but organically at the same time.

CONCLUSION

The ultimate conclusion to be drawn from the entire discussion is that social work needs a new paradigm, one more in line with the scientific findings of many fields and also more in harmony with certain values that take social work beyond the egoism of individualism.

The presentation of one such paradigm constitutes the remainder of this book. This new paradigm rests fundamentally on the proposition that whatever else can be said about the human condition, the irreducible state of human life is membership.

REFERENCES

Arnold, H., & Bloom, T. (1981). Institutional change as a creative process: Some educational and practice considerations. *Journal of Social Work Process, 19,* 4–24.

Balgopal, P.R., & Vassil, T.V. (1983). *Groups in social work: An ecological perspective.* New York: Macmillan.

Bloom, M. (1983). Empirically based clinical research. In A. Rosenblatt & D. Waldfogel (Eds.), *Handbook of clinical social work* (pp. 560–582). San Francisco: Jossey-Bass.

Boehm, W. (1959). The nature of social work. *Social Work, 3* (2), 10–18.

Bowers, S. (1949). The nature and definition of social casework (Parts I, II, III). *Journal of Social Casework, 30* (8, 9, 10), 311–317, 369–375, 412–417.

Carlton, T.O. (1984). *Clinical social work in health settings: A guide to professional practice with exemplars.* New York: Springer Publishing Co.

Carlton, T.O. (1986). Group process and group work in health social work practice. *Social Work with Groups, 9* (2), 5–20.

Chatterjee, P. (1984). Cognitive theories in social work practice. *Social Service Review, 58* (1), 63–80.

Clemenger, F. (1980). Review of the life model of social work practice, by C.B. Germain & A. Gitterman. *Journal of Education for Social Work, 16* (3), 121–122.

Compton, B.R., & Galloway, B. (1984). *Social work processes* (3rd ed.). Homewood, IL: Dorsey Press.

Coulton, C.J. (1981). Person–environment fits as a focus in health care. *Social Work, 26* (1), 26–35.

Coyle, G.L. (1947). *Group experience and democratic values.* New York: Women's Press.

Coyle, G.L. (1948). *Group work and American youth.* New York: Harper & Row.

Durkheim, E. (1982). *The rules of sociological method.* S. Lukes (Ed.) (pp. 50–59). New York: The Free Press.

Ell, K. (1984). Social networks, social supports, and health status: A review. *Social Service Review, 58* (1), 133–349.

Fischer, J. (1976). *The effectiveness of social casework.* Springfield, IL: Charles C. Thomas.

Garvin, C.D., & Seabury, B. (1984). *Interpersonal practices in social work: Process and procedures.* Englewood Cliffs, NJ: Prentice-Hall.

Germain, C.B. (1976). Time, an ecological variable in social work practice. *Social Casework, 57* (7), 419–426.

Germain, C.B. (1977). An ecological perspective on social work practice in health care. *Social Work in Health Care, 3* (1), 67–76.

Germain, C.B. (1978). Space, an ecological variable in social work practice. *Social Casework, 59* (9), 515–522.

Germain, C.B. (1979). *Social work practice: People and environments.* New York: Columbia University Press.

Germain, C.B. (1980). Social context of clinical social work. *Social Work, 25* (6), 483–488.

Germain, C.B. (1984). *Social work practice in health care: An ecological perspective.* New York: The Free Press.

Germain, C.B. (1986). The place of community work with an ecological approach to social work practice. In S. Taylor & R.W. Roberts (Eds.), *Theories and practice of community social work* (pp. 30–55). New York: Columbia University Press.

Germain, C.B. (1985). Work with the community and the organization in child welfare practice. In J. Laird & A. Hartman (Eds.), *Handbook of child welfare.* New York: The Free Press.

Germain, C.B., & Gitterman, A. (1980). *The life model of social work practice.* New York: Columbia University Press.

Glasser, P., Sarri, R., & Vinter, V. (1984). *Individual change through small groups.* New York: The Free Press.

Hamilton, G. (1940). *Theory and practice of social case work.* New York: Columbia University Press.

Hearn, G. (1958). *Theory building in social work.* Toronto: University of Toronto Press.

Hollis, F. (1964). *Casework: A psychosocial therapy.* New York: Columbia University Press.

Hollis, F., & Woods, M.E. (1981). *Casework: A psychosocial therapy* (3rd ed.). New York: Columbia University Press.

Kagle, J.D., & Cowger, C.D. (1984). Blaming the client: Implicit agenda in practice research? *Social Work, 29* (4), 347–351.

Krill, D.F. (1979). Existential social work. In F. Turner (Ed.), *Social work treatment—Interlocking theoretical approaches* (2nd ed.) (pp. 147–176). New York: The Free Press.

Lonergan, E.C. (1985). *Group intervention: How to begin and maintain groups in medical and psychiatric settings.* New York: Jason Aronson.

Mahler, M., Pines, F., & Bergman, A. (1975). *The psychological birth of the human infant.* New York: Basic Books.

Meyer, C. (1970). *Social work practice—A response to the urban crisis.* New York: The Free Press.

National Association of Social Workers. (1977). Code of ethics. In J.B.

Turner (Ed.), *Encyclopedia of social work* (17th ed.) (Vol. II) (pp. 1066–1067). New York: Author.

National Association of Social Workers. (1983). Code of ethics. In *1983–1984 supplement to the encyclopedia of social work* (17th ed.) (pp. 257–262). New York: Author.

Northen, H. (1969). *Social work in groups.* New York: Columbia University Press.

Perlman, H.H. (1957). *Social casework—A problem-solving process.* Chicago: University of Chicago Press.

Phillips, D.C. (1976). *Holistic thought in social science.* Stanford: Stanford University Press.

Phillips, H.U. (1957). *Essentials of social group work skill.* New York: Association Press.

Pincus, A., & Minahan, A. (1973). *Social work practice: Model and method.* Itasca, IL: F.E. Peacock.

Pray, K.L.M. (1949). *Social work in a revolutionary age.* Philadelphia: University of Pennsylvania Press.

Reamer, F.C. (1983). The free-will determinism debate in social work. *Social Service Review, 57* (4), 627–644.

Richmond, M. (1917). *Social diagnosis.* New York: Russell Sage Foundation.

Roberts, R.W., & Northen, H. (Eds.). (1976). *Theories of social work with groups.* New York: Columbia University Press.

Robinson, V.P. (1943). *Training for skill in social case work.* Philadelphia: Pennsylvania School of Social Work.

Ryder, E. (1976). The functional approach. In R.W. Roberts & H. Northen (Eds.), *Theories of social work with groups* (pp. 153–170). New York: Columbia University Press.

Schild, S., & Black, R.B. (1984). *Social work and genetics: A guide for practice.* New York: Haworth Press.

Schlesinger, E.G. (1958). *Health care social work practice: Concepts and strategies.* St. Louis: C.V. Mosby.

Schwartz, W. (1961). The social worker in the group. In *New perspectives on services to groups: Theory, organization, practice.* New York: National Association of Social Workers.

Schwartz, W. (1976). Between client and system: The mediating function. In R.W. Roberts & H. Northen (Eds.), *Theories of social work with groups* (pp. 171–197). New York: Columbia University Press.

Schwartz, W., & Zalba, S.R. (1971). *The practice of group work.* New York: Columbia University Press.

Shulman, L. (1984). *The skills of helping individuals and groups* (2nd ed.). Itasca, IL: F.E. Peacock.

Smalley, R.E. (1967). *Theory for social work practice.* New York: Columbia University Press.

Stein, I. (1974). *Systems theory, science, and social work.* Metuchen, NJ: The Scarecrow Press.

Stewart, R.P. (1985). From the president. *NASW News, 30* (5), 2.

Strean, H. (1979). *Psychoanalytic theory and casework practice.* New York: The Free Press.

Swift, L. (1946). *A social worker's creed.* New York: Family Service Association of America.

Taft, J. (1944). *A functional approach to family case work.* Philadelphia: Pennsylvania School of Social Work.

Toseland, R.W., & Rivas, R.F. (1984). *An introduction to group work practice.* New York: Macmillan Publishing Company.

Turner, F.J. (Ed.). (1979). *Social work treatment—Interlocking theoretical approaches* (2nd ed.). New York: The Free Press.

Van der Veelde, C. (1985). Body images of one's self and of others: Developmental and clinical significance. *American Journal of Psychiatry, 142,* 527–537.

Weick, A. (1984). The concept of responsibility in a health model of social work. *Social Work in Health Care, 10* (2), 13–25.

Wilson, G., & Ryland, G. (1949). *Social group work practice.* Boston: Houghton Mifflin.

Winters, W.G., & Easton, F. (1983). *The practice of social work in schools: An ecological perspective.* New York: The Free Press.

Younghusband, E.L. (1979). Foreword. In F.J. Turner (Ed.), *Social work treatment—Interlocking theoretical approaches* (2nd ed.) (pp. xiii–xiv). New York: The Free Press.

2 The Membership Perspective of Human Behavior

The major reason that social workers need to be concerned about the formulation of human behavior knowledge is that social work helps to bring about changes in many aspects of daily life. What is desired, therefore, are conceptual formulations that are comprehensive and valid, that take into account the interventive tasks social workers are expected to perform.

Carefully constructed models and scientific perspectives have the advantage of parsimony (Berger, 1986; Fawcett & Downs, 1986). Each word and each sentence count. The justification of any model or perspective is the contribution it makes to the entire undertaking. What is required is a lean picture, one that assumes that each practitioner fills in the specifics needed to make it practical and useful. With such an approach, resting as it does on phenomena as complex as those that describe human behavior, however, there always exists the danger of oversimplification.

Despite this danger and its potential deficits, it is possible to present a perspective that accounts, in principle, for the functions of the body, social interaction, the assignment of meaning of the human experience, and the internalization of relationships in order to build and maintain the ego. Through it, one repeatedly discovers a certain unity that many aspects of life portray with surprising consistency. In other words, the membership perspective involves certain predictable constants. Everything within it is componential; nothing is merely a part. The whole stays intact at every level of discourse, from the highest to the lowest level of abstraction. The concepts that portray this unity are *member* and its derivatives, *membership* and *membership behavior.* The term member implies other members, and it is this core condition that makes the membership perspective different from all other social work perspectives.

The concept of member rules out individualism with the same energy with which it rejects collectivism. It neither locates life's core in the physical nor in the psychological or the social alone. Instead it holds that the member is a functioning human being, a component of a world full of people. Membership is treasured and protected as indispensable to the life of the human community.

THE MEMBER

Every person is a member. A member is a human being characterized by body, personality, sociality, and the ability to comprehend human experience. Every member is an element in the community of men and women (Lipowski, 1984; Woodger, 1952).

The term member refers to a person who is:

1. A physical being bounded by semipermeable membranes and cavities;
2. A social being in continuous interaction with others who are both seen and unseen (Falck, 1981); and
3. A psychological being capable of private experience.

The fact that in speaking of member one implicitly speaks of others, who are also members, leads to the following inferences:

1. A member's actions are socially derived and contributory;
2. The identity of each member is bound up with that of others through social involvement;
3. A member is a person whose differences from others creates tensions that lead to growth, group cohesion, and group conflict; and
4. Human freedom is defined by simultaneous concern for oneself and others (Falck, 1976).

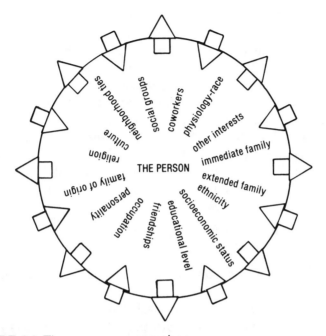

FIGURE 2.1 The person as member.
Source: From *Clinical social work in health settings* (p. 28), T.O. Carlton, Ed., 1984. New York: Springer Publishing Co. Reprinted by permission.

The individual and the member share a common characteristic: Both refer to one person. The difference between them is that an individual can exist separately from others; the member cannot.

In Figure 2.1 a schematic representation of the member is presented. It will be noted that the person as member is linked to others as a basic condition, not by choice. Also, the linkages to others imply a variety of purposes. One could add other purposes, yet the principle of connectedness appears clear from the outset.

MEMBERSHIP

Any consideration of membership must address the conditions that define it. In practical terms one may well ask, who is and who is not a member? Or the question may be posed in terms of the circumstances of membership (e.g., where it begins and ends, or even in terms of the laws that can help us to understand membership).

Boundaries have to do with distinctions between the self and the other. They differentiate between the intrapsychic and the interpersonal. They denote where things begin and end. They illuminate the processes of interchange between one thing and another. Boundaries describe the conditions of access, egress, and limits. If one can state what principles operate within what kinds of boundaries, one can also test for their universality and their limitations.

Statements about boundaries help us define membership. There are certain common characteristics that apply to all statements about membership. These can be expressed in two boundary principles: constant connectedness and conditional accessibility.

The First Boundary Principle: Constant Connectedness

The Principle of Constant Connectedness states that all components of wholes are permanently linked by virtue of common need, function, and prerequisites for survival. This principle expresses the fact that from conception to death the human being links all his or her components to others, as well as to nonliving things. Despite outward appearances, there are no empty spaces between and among members.

The principle of constant connectedness derives from empirical observations and findings from neurology, anatomy, neuroanatomy, biology, audiology, and other fields (Fletcher & Evans, 1983; Verney & Kelly, 1981). These findings indicate that all elements of the human body are linked in componential ways and that all people are components of other people. Member and membership are componential concepts; they are holistic and all-inclusive (Falck, 1984).

Membership is permanent. It cannot be reversed. Constant connectedness is, therefore, a powerful notion. Because most theorists conceptualize the relationships of a person as external to that person, however, the power of this boundary principle is generally overlooked. Yet one cannot resign from one's memberships. Their permanence pushes itself into conscious thought in "surprising, fleeting thoughts, in feelings, in intrusive, sudden reminders" (Falck, 1980, p. 24). This happens when people meet others they have known earlier and are reminded that they were part of one another in the past and are part of one another again in the present, "whatever the consequences may be."

Even when one loses someone through death, the membership of the survivor with the deceased cannot be unexperienced; its meaning is only "modified into a past tense" (Falck, 1980, p. 23). The same is true when couples divorce and when children leave the parental home.

Social arrangements and social roles also indicate permanence because they are relatively constant. Moreover, they explain *how* people are connected to one another (e.g., husbands and wives, parents and children, teachers and students). The principle of constant connectedness, then, denotes permanence in time, meaning, and process.

The Second Boundary Principle: Conditional Accessibility

The Principle of Conditional Accessibility holds that the nature of access from one member to another is subject to specifiable conditions (i.e., selectivity). Access is governed by rules that both facilitate and restrict it. These may be physical or structural, or they may be functional in a nonphysical sense. In the first case, one may think of cells and their membranes; in the second, of social interaction. There is no access when boundaries are closed. Figure 2.2, Constant Connectedness and Conditional Accessibility, illustrates the nature of boundaries in the membership perspective. Where there are no boundaries, merger occurs and one is unable to distinguish anything from anything else. In such situations, boundary and conditionality of access do not exist and symbiotic merger results. Such symbiotic merger is a serious psychopathology (Chatham, 1985; Rinsley, 1977; Sarwer-Forner, 1977; Takahashi, 1980). Where there are solid boundaries between components—in reality an impossible condition—no life can take place.

Silverman, Lachmann, and Millich (1982) studied symbiotic merger among adults and the ability of the same persons to develop a sense of self. Their findings yield the hypothesis that "unconscious oneness fantasies can enhance adaptation *if, simultaneously, a sense of self can be preserved*" (p. 1, emphasis added). Mahler, Bergman, and Pine (1975) found that the development of the healthy human ego

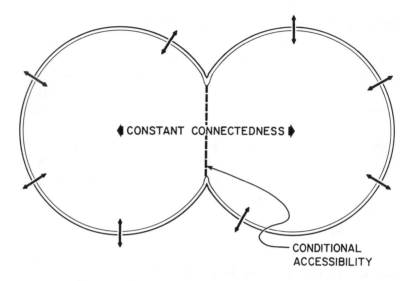

FIGURE 2.2 Constant connectedness and conditional accessibility.

in small children, upon which the growing self rests, is a dynamic process in which the child moves in phaselike ways toward autonomy within the relationship with the mother. The fact of the relationship does not change as the child grows into an adult and the mother grows older, but the psychological quality of the relationship does change. Kernberg (1975) offers a similar view. Should, for a variety of reasons, this normal process of ego development either fail to occur or occur inadequately, the memberships of the person involved will still exist, but they will be pathological. The literature on borderline conditions underlines and strengthens the etiological implications of this view (Chatham, 1985; Kernberg, 1975; Masterson & Rinsley, 1975; Rinsley, 1982).

Normal membership describes the middle way in which mature relationships with others and a clear sense of self are the unitary products that arise from the same sources. The constancy of such balanced experiences, internalized by each person, offers a sense of being related with and to others because one is a well-functioning self.

The conclusion is that membership, regardless of quality, is expressed in the constant connectedness of people. Early in life, it mainly involves mother and child, but membership is constant throughout life. At any given time, the emerging and emerged self reflects a quality of membership that declares, as it were, one's satisfactions and dissatisfactions, all the positive and negative links of persons to each other. At work is a selective process, conditional accessibility. It is open-ended and, therefore, subject both to reinforcement and to change.

MEMBERSHIP BEHAVIOR

Four human functions describe the content and the analytic power of the two principles of the membership perspective. Each of the four captures a dimension of human behavior. All lend themselves to a considerable degree of empirical observation: biological process in the human body, social process in interaction, symbolization through the demonstration of meanings attached to behavior, and psychological processes through the operationalization of psychoanalytic concepts. All are subject to analysis and explanation through the application of the principle of constant connectedness and the principle of conditional accessibility.

Membership in Biology: Physical Functioning

Physical functioning refers to all behaviors of the human body. All components of the body are interlinked, directly and indirectly. The principle of conditional accessibility operates throughout the body through its many specialized behaviors. Intra- and intercellular functioning is selective and is guided, if not determined, by the structure of cells, the transport mechanisms within the membranes of single cells, and their relationships to entire organs. In biology, conditional accessibility may be illustrated by the semipermeability of the cell membranes that allow passage of selected molecules and prevent that of others (Bretscher, 1985; Critchley, 1978; Fawcett, 1966).

A further example of the membership principles of constant connectedness and conditional accessibility is found in the operation of the so-called "blood–brain barrier," which is needed to provide the brain with a steady enough state to function in a constant fashion. To accomplish this, the rest of the body and particularly the blood are separated from the brain, but not absolutely so. Goldstein and Betz (1986) describe this process as follows:

> [T]he brain must be rigorously isolated from transient changes in the composition of the blood.
> [H]ow is this feat accomplished? The answer lies in the unique structure of the capillaries that supply blood to the tissues of the brain. The cells of the brain capillaries, unlike those of other capillaries, form a continuous wall that prevents many substances from entering the brain. The uninterrupted capillary wall provides the basis of the blood–brain barrier whose existence was first demonstrated conclusively in the 1960s. By cordoning off the brain from the other tissues, the barrier serves a critical function. Yet if the isolation were complete, the brain would die for lack of nourishment. Fortunately the essential nutrients traverse the blood–brain barrier easily, helped across by transport systems that recognize specific molecules and carry them into the brain.
> [T]he transport systems not only bring nutrients into the brain but also pump surplus substances out, thereby helping to maintain a constant environment for the neurons. (p. 74)

The significance of this process is of the highest importance for the maintenance of life. It occurs under controlled conditions internal to the human body. In this sense, the process is self-regulating (cf. Piaget, 1968) within a semipermeable situation. That is, while the blood–brain barrier is fixed in one sense, it is not completely so. Were this not the case, the exchange process to which Goldstein and Betz refer in the quotation above would not occur and although the brain would be protected from the rest of the body, the lack of exchange would obviously destroy the person.

What is fundamentally involved is the constant contact between the brain and the rest of the body under conditions that control their connectedness, that is, selectivity. As we have shown, cellular structure and the blood–brain barrier provide major evidence for the biological documentation for the membership construct.

Membership as Social Process: Interaction

Social functioning refers to the ability of members to interact with others. Usually thought of as mostly verbal in nature and content, social interaction also includes nonverbal elements that vary in type, style, culturally approved means, and purpose. The survival of members is determined in irreducible ways by the presence of social interaction, regardless of type and specific content. The principle of constant connectedness captures this state. The constancy does not necessarily mean that it must be physically demonstrated at all times, nor that it must always be of a particular, predetermined, or fixed type. It does mean, however, that because there is human contact, the member knows that he or she is a member even though the interaction may range from loving to destructive.

Levinger (1983) describes the membership of a husband and wife over time. Beginning with their first meeting, he recounts their initial attraction, the building of their relationship, their marriage, the gradual deterioration of their relationship, and its ending. In his description of this couple, it is possible to see the membership principles of constant connectedness and conditional accessibility at work in the form of an intimate relationship. Selected citations from his description of its various phases make this clear.

Levinger first recounts the couple's first meeting, initial attraction, and the building of their relationship as remembered by the wife, Susan.

> *First Meeting*
> I first met Tom in Paris in 1955. . . . Tom had already finished college. . . . I remember that neither of us made any effort to talk to the other. . . . [H]e registered very little in my awareness.
> *Initial Attraction*
> It wasn't until Christmas break, three months later, that I again noticed Tom. . . . [W]e spent a lively evening together. . . .
> *Building the Relationship*
> We didn't see each other again until I returned two weeks later. But something had blossomed. . . . A month later I moved in with Tom. . . . Well, we surprised our parents when we wrote them that we would get married. . . . (pp. 315–318)

Levinger continues the recounting of the relationship describing the early years of the marriage, the completion of Susan's education, the development of Tom's (the husband) career as an architect, the birth of their three children, and Susan's return to law school when their oldest child was eight. It is at the point that Susan completes her legal education that the deterioration of their relationship becomes apparent, as Tom remembers.

Deterioration
[W]hen she graduated, she was offered a job with a fine law firm and I think she wanted to take it. . . . I had taken on new responsibilities as a head partner and needed extra help at home to entertain colleagues and clients. I asked her if she would postpone taking a full-time job and she agreed to wait. . . .

That their relationship continued to deteriorate is made clear in the recounting of the events surrounding a dinner at which Susan received an award in recognition of her volunteer work with Legal Aid. Susan remembers.

I was very embarrassed when Tom never showed up at the banquet; the chair reserved next to me near the center of the head table stayed empty all evening. I was even angrier when I returned home that night to discover him watching TV and to hear him tell me that he had been just too tired to attend the dinner. That incident brought matters into focus.

Ending
Finally, I figured I'd had enough. I received another good job offer and decided to take it without consulting Tom. I also told Tom that I'd probably want to separate from him. When I told him he seemed stunned. (pp. 315–318)

In these excerpts from Levinger's description of an intimate relationship, the membership perspective of human behavior is portrayed in rather dramatic fashion. The themes appear with considerable clarity. In a period of about 15 years, Tom and Susan developed a mutual membership that was marked by permanence (constant connectedness), yet variable in nature, content, and quality (conditional accessibility). It was obviously meaningful to both partners through courtship, marriage, and the birth of their three children. What changed was the quality of their membership beginning about the time Susan returned to school for her legal education. Highly positive in the early period, their relationship deteriorated in later years. When Susan left Tom, its former qualities were hardly recognizable.

Although Levinger conceptualizes the last phase of this marriage as an ending, the membership perspective holds that the membership of Susan and Tom continues, albeit under very different circumstances. The internalization of object relations makes it possible to see that although the qualities of their membership are modified by the physical separation, it is not ended. Internalized object relations take membership relations beyond social and biological interaction (Falck, 1976, 1978, 1980).

In sum, the principle of conditional accessibility expresses the fact that social interaction is highly selective, and this selectivity shapes the conduct of most human relationships. Social rules, as reflected in law, tradition, ethics, morals, and many other social conventions, document the finely tuned and highly focused selectivity in human interaction that the principle addresses. Conditional accessibility and constant connectedness work together to make social interaction both possible and effective. They contribute to getting the tasks of everyday life done and also to the exceptional joys and sorrows that are part of the sense of wholeness one feels as a member among members.

Membership as Meaning: Symbolization

A third characteristic of membership is symbolization (i.e., the fact that members attach meaning to their own behavior and to the behavior of others). Symbolization is constant and selective at the same time.

The principle of constant connectedness expresses itself in the monitoring that takes place when persons observe their own behavior and the behavior of others. In the process of trying to understand what it is they see and hear, they endow the behavior observed with culturally agreed upon meanings. It is this assignment of meaning that enables members to demonstrate their connectedness.

Conditional accessibility determines the *kinds* of meanings members attach to their experiences. The choices are determined by the symbols made available to members by the cultural pool within the limits specified by the culture itself. This is to say, cultures provide their members with a variety of optional symbols. These differ from culture to culture and, within certain limits, from subculture to subculture. Members of such groups use these symbols to communicate with themselves and with others in languages understood by all or nearly all in any given cultural community (Berger, 1966).

The symbolization factor of membership is important because it accounts in large part for how and why particular people learn to interpret the verbal and nonverbal content of human interaction in particular ways. Symbolization is based first on the occurrence of events (what happens) and second on reactions to events (what they mean). In the first instance, one assumes that anyone can witness an event and describe it in ways similar to the descriptions of other witnesses (i.e., objectively). In the second, the assumption is that each member understands and interprets events in idiosyncratic ways (i.e., subjectively). Symbolization thus explains why single standards rarely exist that cut across different cultures and cultural subgroups and signify agreed-upon meanings of behavior.

One example of symbolization is found in the expressed attitude of many Americans toward aging, often stated in negative terms. Some older people speak of themselves as wasted, pushed aside, treated as no longer useful, even of actively being mistreated by their children and others. The perception is that the meaning of aging is similar to being thrown out with the rubbish. And, since rubbish is not saved but is eliminated, older people sometimes liken themselves to the symbolic meanings of rubbish and transfer these meanings to nursing homes or homes for the aged. In American culture, these meanings suggest that such places are places where one waits to die. The central issue here is not the number of one's years, but in the meanings that accompany them.

The work of Erikson (1959) on human aging is helpful in understanding symbolization from the membership perspective. Erikson's well-known conceptualization of the human life cycle consists of eight stages. One of these, integrity versus despair and disgust, corresponds to that period in human life usually designated as the time of aging. In Eriksonian theory, this period is anticipated by all of the stages that precede it.

Erikson defines integrity as:

[T]he acceptance of one's own and only life cycle and of the people who have become significant to it as something that had to be and that, by necessity, permitted no other substitutions. It thus means a different love for one's parents, free of the wish that they should have been different, and an acceptance of the fact that one's life is one's own responsibility. (p. 98)

The only modification of Erikson's definition required by the membership perspective would be recognition of the fact that one's life is one's own responsibility *as an irrevocable member of the human community.* Erikson continues:

> [T]he lack or loss of this accrued ego integration is signified by despair and an often unconscious fear of death; the one and only life cycle that is not accepted as the ultimate of life. Despair expresses the feeling that the time is short, too short for the attempt to start another life and to try out alternate roads to integrity. Such despair is often hidden behind a show of disgust. . . (p. 98)

Nearly two decades after this initial formulation, Erikson (1976) expanded his integrity versus despair and disgust stage by adding "wisdom" to it. He defined wisdom as "the detached and yet active concern with human life itself in the face of death itself" and held that wisdom "maintains and conveys the integrity of experience in spite of the decline of bodily and mental functions" (p. 23). Thus, Erikson's conceptualization demonstrates the principle of constant connectedness in the sense that he views the responses of people in this and other life stages in relation to life experiences involving themselves and others.

Through the use of evaluative language, such as "integrity" (good), "despair" and "disgust" (undesirable), "wisdom" (highly desirable), and "acceptance" (maturity), Erikson assigns value-laden meanings to a wide range of behaviors. Thus, he more than describes human behavior in epigenetic terms; he also *interprets* (symbolizes) it in terms that are meaningful in Western culture and thereby demonstrates the principle of conditional accessibility.

Erikson's theory suggests a rather orderly progression through the various stages of the life cycle. Not all developmental theorists accept this view, however. Riley (1978), for example, does not see the life course as fixed. She holds that the behavioral expectations for each life stage are neither prescribed nor preordained. The basis for these conclusions is Riley's observation that both the nature and meanings of life events vary throughout the life cycle, "not only with the changing nature of the family, the school, the workplace, the community, but also with changing ideas, values, and beliefs" (p. 39). Similarly, Neugarten (1979) suggests that changes in adulthood reflect the slow accumulation of life events and "the continuities and discontinuities in conscious preoccupations," which are influenced by "perceptions of change in the significant people with whom we interact" (p. 892).

Irrespective of the degree of flexibility or orderliness in these and other developmental theories, however, the fact is that no major life events occur without symbolization. Aging is not just the accumulation of years on a calendar. Rather, it derives its significance for the specific member who is "aging" and the others with whom the aging person shares membership from the meanings they ascribe to growing older.

In summary, symbolization is a constant process. Its nature and qualities change as members change throughout life. That is, people attach meanings to life events throughout their lives, and these meanings are the basis on which important decisions affecting their lives are made. Symbolization in other words is not arbitrary. It takes place under a combination of social and psychological conditions that allow experience to be endowed with meaning (Blumer, 1969).

Membership as Intrapsychic Process: Internalization

The internalization of object relations forms the bridge from external reality to internal reality. In this statement, external reality refers to interaction with others. Internal reality, in turn, refers to the phenomenon of making these relationships an aspect of one's inner life. The meanings of internalized relationships, especially those absorbed in the early stages of life, appear to be of crucial importance to the nature and quality of further psychological development. This is because they are available to the person for active use through recall and in the unconscious are the basis for a variety of purposes, often of a repetitive nature, long after their internalization first took place. They are, therefore, of crucial importance to the formation of the ego and the development of a healthy and effective personality (Kernberg, 1976; Schafer, 1968).

The most influential of psychoanalytic object-relations theorists is Otto F. Kernberg, whose seminal work (1976) contains several points germane to membership as intrapsychic process:

> In the broadest terms, psychoanalytic object-relations theory represents the psychoanalytic study of the nature and origin of interpersonal relations, and the nature and origin of intrapsychic structures deriving from fixating, modifying, and reactivating past social relations. Psychoanalytic object-relations theory focuses upon the internalization of interpersonal relations, their contribution to normal and pathological ego and superego developments, and the mutual influences of intrapsychic and interpersonal object relations. (p. 56)

Kernberg notes that the term "object" refers to "human object" and that this meaning reflects its traditional use in psychoanalytic metapsychology to refer to "relations with others" (p. 58). He notes further that the focus in psychoanalytic object-relations theory is on five specific criteria: (1) "the depth and stability of internal relations with others; (2) the tolerance of ambivalence toward loved objects; (3) the capacity for tolerating guilt and separation and for the working through of depressive crises; (4) the extent to which the self-concept is integrated; and (5) the extent to which behavior patterns correspond to the self-concept" (p. 59).

Because the internalization of object relations is a private, mental process, it cannot be observed directly. It can, however, be studied indirectly. The most obvious way to study this process is to interview people. This approach, however, is the most unreliable one from a scientific standpoint. The more scientific, and therefore more reliable, approach is to develop a series of stimulus situations to which a person responds. This approach has the advantage of removing the observer from the relationship. Major examples of this latter approach are the Structural Analysis of Social Behavior (SASB and INTREX) developed by Benjamin (1986a, b).

The SASB and INTREX consist of a series of questions that yield information on 108 dimensions of relationships between the respondent and others (e.g., mother, father). The questions these instruments pose are designed specifically to elicit data on the meanings of the respondent's internalized relationships with others. It is as if the respondent member asks, "What do I remember about so and so and me?" "What do I remember about us?" "What did it feel like at the time, as I remember it now?" Thus, the SASB and INTREX bring significant interpersonal and intrapsychic experience into current consciousness. Their significance from the membership perspective is that they constitute an operational definition of personality dynamics.

The advantage that object-relations theory holds for the elucidation of the membership perspective is that it accounts for both personality and social functioning in the form of a single continuum. This formulation of psychoanalytic theory is integrative in that it describes important aspects of social and psychological functioning simultaneously (Falck, 1980).

The principle of constant connectedness appears in the fact that internalization is lifelong. Thus, new object relations are internalized and old ones are both reinforced and modified. Object relations address not only the images a given member might have of other members, but also the cognitive and the affective aspects of such relationships. The cognitive aspect deals with the facts of relationship, such as persons involved, time, place, words, and circumstances. The affective deals with feelings that are involved in them. Feelings range the entire spectrum of human emotion from love and hate, to anger and joy, to disgust and stimulation. A typical example is the man who, at age 50, remembers a teacher he had in childhood who loved him, but about whom he remembers little else. He has even forgotten the subject the teacher taught, but in his mind's eye he can see him. His present feelings about him are warm and affectionate. He refers to him as his favorite teacher. Another example is the 63-year-old client who feels that if his now-deceased mother had known that her granddaughter had an active sex life at age 16, she might have been ashamed—not only of the granddaughter, but of her son who thought no better of his own mother than to permit his daughter such leeway. The feeling is one of guilt over the nature of the mother's (grandmother's) relationships with the son (father).

Internalization is subject to control by the ego (A. Freud, 1937). It is not so much a question of admitting or not admitting the object relations being internalized as it is a matter of selective shaping. Bellak, Hurvich, and Gediman (1973) describe how the ego performs these selective functions, admitting, rejecting, and distorting. It is this function of the ego that allows the person to perform psychically to the maximum extent possible. Moreover, it is this selective function of the ego that provides evidence that the principle of conditional accessibility is active in intrapsychic process. The ego always manages inputs from the id and other sources through its monitoring and self-protective selectivity.

THE QUALITIES OF MEMBERSHIP BEHAVIOR

The principle of constant connectedness speaks to the fact of membership, but it does not address the qualitative aspects of membership directly. Yet, it is in these aspects that the most significant consequences of the membership perspective are discovered. The qualities of membership can be classified according to three types: positive, negative, and ambiguous.

Positive Membership

Positive memberships satisfy. They elaborate the member's abilities to interact with others in gratifying ways that reflect the fact that others wish one well and demonstrate appreciation for one's talents and achievements. Such memberships suggest that it is untrue that one stands alone. Rather, they suggest that one's birth, life, and death do make a difference to others. The fact that members of families share the same surname, for example, speaks to the "we" aspects of the "I."

In creative and positive membership, the sense of belonging is a source of security for the member whose behavior makes a difference that is treasured both by self and others. This sense of belonging is not confined to childhood but extends throughout the person's life. Even when a member becomes emancipated from others, as when grown children leave parents, the implied separation takes place within the membership of the family or similar group (Erikson, 1959; Mahler et al., 1975). There is knowledge that the price one pays when one becomes an identifiable self does not include giving up one's fundamental membership with those one treasures.

Thus, when the qualities of membership are positive, the elaboration of one's sense of being a self is fed and supported by others. Being a self is a source of pride for those with whom membership is shared, as well as for the self. This idealized condition is what new parents, church members, school members, lovers, indeed all involved in positive memberships are most likely to experience.

Negative Membership

Negative memberships, too, are statements about the qualities of human relationships. Feelings of alienation, in particular, split the fact of membership from the *perception* of membership. It is a fact that people are members; it is also a fact that thousands of people perceive that they are not. Given economic desperation, such people become the underclass of society, and, feeling disconnected, they lack confidence in what they perceive to be unfair social structures and arrangements. Consequently, they often act on the belief that no one owes them and they owe no one.

Negative membership perception is not limited to the economic underclass, however, or even to minorities of color. The first boundary principle, constant connectedness, makes it clear that the poor, minorities of color, Jews, Native Americans, the mentally ill, and innumerable others are members like anyone else. The questions always are, "Do we really belong? Are we perceived and accepted as full and equal members?" In terms of the principle of conditional accessibility, the answer is generally affirmative, but it is within this consideration that serious problems arise.

These problems are usually the products of power, of the advantages that accrue to some out of the sufferings of others, of the self-interested maintenance of values that reinforce existing social arrangements. Often, these situations are abetted by an inability or an unwillingness of those suffering from the problematic situation to act with determination against the dominant sources of power. While one may conclude that the membership qualities of the dominant and the submissive, the rich and the poor, the majority and the minorities of color, are essentially stable, this stability does not mean justice, nor does it imply that all is well. Nevertheless, it must also be recognized that one is a member in one's suffering, inequality, and victimization.

The nature of social arrangements, however, is not always the only consideration, or even the main consideration in the determination of membership quality. Immediate personal phenomena such as illness and disability can also determine the quality of one's membership. Permanent disability, for example, is not just an event that occurs to a person under particular circumstances at a particular time. It requires major modification of the person's lifestyle that is permanent and often radical in nature. This modification links together the disabled person's new physical state, changed abilities to function socially, new perceptions of the meaning of life, and psychological state so as to bring about a change in the qualities of his or her memberships. In short, while the person's membership remains constant, the conditions of accessibility that govern his or her interactions with others have changed.

Whether any given example of negative membership stems from social injustice, physical disability, or some other set of circumstances, membership remains constant. In the first instance, it is as if fate determines that in one way or another even the most disliked share a common destiny with all others. In the second, the qualities of membership may be radically changed because of disability, but not the fact of membership itself. In both instances, members can influence the qualities of their membership, but not its existence. Thus, while membership is immutable, its qualities are malleable. It is in this flexibility that hope and the anticipation of more humane memberships can be found.

Ambiguous Membership

Not all memberships can be classified as positive or negative. Most are both. Ambiguous membership is always shaded; it always consists of a mixture of qualities. In this middle ground, memberships may be quite positive in some areas of life and less so in others. A member, for example, may do quite well at work, but suffer a painful and problematic home life. One may suffer pain without any realistic hope that it will ever totally subside, and yet accept the pain sufficiently to continue to interact positively with others even when a modification of work hours and type of activity is required. Millions of single-parent families contain members who wish for a less stressful, easier existence and yet manage to rear children, attain educational goals, and meet the demands of daily life successfully.

Human beings must be understood in terms of the particular constellation of their memberships, their qualities, and their predictive potential for change. This requires an honest estimate of what can be changed and what has to remain as is. Such estimates raise serious questions about human suffering and the mutual ability of all members of the community to adapt to it. This is not a rationalization for social injustice. Rather, it is recognition that whatever the qualities of membership may be in any given instance, all members are behaving human beings and as such influence their own lives and the lives of others. Thus, the person whose memberships are ambiguous describes the membership qualities of others with whom he or she interacts. This is also true of the suffering person, whose memberships are negative, and of those whose memberships are satisfying, optimistic, and fulfilling.

BEYOND THE MEMBER

In a society that educates its members to perceive themselves as individuals, the term *member* can be easily distorted and misused. Simply substituting *member* for *individual,* without the other adaptations that need to be made, does not render membership understandable. Nor can it be taken for granted that simply presenting the main ideas of the membership perspective will make the perspective clear to social workers prepared in a different tradition. It is necessary, therefore, to clarify how membership accounts for what other formulations call the group, the social environment, the organization, even the society.

Membership *includes* these additional dimensions of human behavior beyond the one member, because the term "member" implies plurality (i.e., other members). Anything that exists beyond a given member is subject, therefore, to the definition of the member. Thus, membership denotes the continuity that the individual/environment differentiation fails to take into account or clarify.

Figure 2.3, the Membership Grid, represents this continuity in schematic form. Although the Membership Grid is more elaborate than the two-member group illustrated in Figure 2.2, it is still a vastly oversimplified picture of human reality. To take this reality fully into

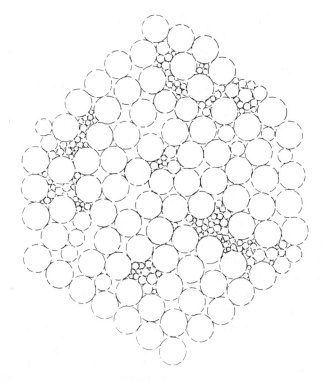

FIGURE 2.3 The membership grid.

account would require a diagram without limits. Its potential size could account for infinite numbers of members. Therefore, even when one places boundaries around the smallest numerical group (the dyad), there are other factors at work that render the boundary delineations as overdetermined, closed, and rigid misrepresentations. The components of the Membership Grid are shown, therefore, with broken boundary lines.

Further examination of the Membership Grid brings additional insights. One of these is that whether one views the diagram as representing an entire society, a family, a small group, or some other membership arrangement, there is an underlying variable at work that characterizes all membership connections. It is the principle of constant connectedness. Were one to add more members to what the Membership Grid represents pictorially, the principle would still hold, *providing the boundary lines remain broken.* These broken boundary lines represent the reciprocal integration of members; that is, the reciprocal integration of any given member with all other members while simultaneously retaining and maintaining his or her differences from all of them in accordance with the principles of membership discussed in this chapter. Potentially, any and all configurations consisting of two or more persons, regardless of the complexities involved, are subject to the same principles.

CONCLUSION

A brief and concise model of human behavior is a fundamental necessity for anyone who wishes to practice a disciplined, professional form of social work. This means that a few concepts must transverse a great amount of intellectual territory. This chapter has presented a perspective that underlies a social work approach that rests on human connectedness rather than on individualism, on human continuities instead of atomism. It views the human being in terms of overlapping physical, social, symbolic, and psychological components of behavior that denote membership as the primary characteristic of all people. This perspective was shown to be neither fortuitous nor accidental. Rather, it was shown to rest on findings from the biological and social sciences on the nature of human beings. These findings indicate a unity that describes all people, a unity that individualism cannot capture or explain.

The more one studies the interaction of human beings, the clearer it becomes that every human member is organized in finely balanced, highly focused, and integrated ways that neither interrupt the constancy of contacts with those physically outside oneself, nor the elements within oneself. This constancy was shown to be discriminatingly regulated in order to assure that the myriad of specialized and qualitative preconditions for human survival are met.

Governed by the principles of constant connectedness and conditional accessibility, membership is the central unifying concept for the whole of human existence. In the chapters that follow, this paradigm of human behavior will be explored further as it is applied in the membership perspective of social work practice.

REFERENCES

Bellak, L., Hurvich, M., & Gediman, H.K. (1973). *Ego functions in schizophrenics, neurotics, and normals.* New York: Wiley.

Benjamin, L.S. (1986a). Adding social and intrapsychic descriptors to axis 1 of DSM III. In T. Millon & G.L. Klerman (Eds.), *Contemporary directions in psychopathology* (pp. 599–638). New York: The Guilford Press.

Benjamin, L.S. (1986b). Operational definition and measurement of dynamics shown in the stream of free association. *Psychiatry: Interpersonal and Biological Processes, 49* (3), 104–129.

Berger, P.L. (1966). *The social construction of reality: A treatise in the sociology of knowledge.* Garden City, NY: Doubleday.

Berger, R.M. (1986). Social work practice models: A better recipe. *Social Casework: The Journal of Contemporary Social Work, 67* (1), 45–54.

Blumer, H. (1969). *Symbolic interactionism: Perspective and method.* Englewood Cliffs, NJ: Prentice-Hall.

Bretscher, M.S. (1985). The molecules of the cell membrane. *Science, 253* (4), 100–108.

Chatham, P. (1985). *Treatment of the borderline personality.* New York: Jason Aronson.

Critchley, M. (1978). *Butterworth's medical dictionary* (2nd ed.). London: Butterworth.

Erikson, E.E. (1959). Identity and the life cycle. *Psychological Issues, 1* (1), 50–100.

Erikson, E.E. (1976). Reflections on Dr. Bork's life cycle. *Daedalus, 185* (2), 1–28.

Falck, H.S. (1976). Individualism and communalism: Two or one? *Social Thought, II* (3), 27–44.

Falck, H.S. (1978). The individuality–groupness effect: Phenomenology, social values and clinical applications. *Social Thought, IV* (3), 29–49.

Falck, H.S. (1980). Aspects of membership: On the integration of psychoanalytic object-relations theory and small group science. *Social Thought, VI* (1), 17–26.

Falck, H.S. (1981). *The "seen" and the "unseen" group in clinical social work practice.* Monograph #3 in the social work practice series. Richmond, VA: Virginia Organization of Health Care Social Workers.

Falck, H.S. (1984). *Peptides as behavior: A psychosomatic approach to peptide research.* Paper presented at the Department of Anatomy, University of Heidelburg, Federal Republic of Germany.

Fawcett, D.W. (1966). *An atlas of fine structure: The cell, its organelles and inclusions.* New York: W.B. Saunders.

Fawcett, J., & Downs, F.S. (1986). *The relationship of theory and research.* Norwalk, CT: Appleton-Century-Crofts.

Fletcher, J.C., & Evans, M.I. (1983). Maternal bonding in early fetal ultra-sound examinations. *New England Journal of Medicine, 308* (7), 392–393.

Freud, A. (1937). *The ego and the mechanisms of defense.* London: Hogarth.

Goldstein, G.W., & Betz, A.L. (1986). The blood–brain barrier. *Scientific American, 255* (3), 74–83.

Kernberg, O.F. (1975). *Borderline conditions and pathological narcissism.* New York: Jason Aronson.

Kernberg, O.F. (1976). *Object-relations theory and clinical psychoanalysis.* New York: Jason Aronson.

Levinger, G. (1983). Development and change. In H.H. Kelley, E. Berscheid, A. Christensen, J.H. Harvey, T.L. Huston, G. Levinger, E. McClintock, L.A. Peplau, & D.R. Peterson, *Close relationships.* New York: W.H. Freeman.

Lipkowski, Z.J. (1984). What does the word "psychosomatic" really mean? An historical and semantic inquiry. *Psychosomatic Medicine, 46* (2), 153–171.

Mahler, M., Bergman, A., & Pine, F. (1975). *The psychological birth of the human infant.* New York: Basic Books.

Masterson, J.F., & Rinsley, D.B. (1975). The borderline syndrome: The role of the mother in the genesis and psychic structure of the borderline personality. *International Journal of Psychoanalysis, 56* (1), 163–177.

Neugarten, B.L. (1979). Time, age, and the life cycle. *American Journal of Psychiatry, 136* (7), 887–894.

Piaget, J. (1968). *Structuralism.* New York: Harper and Row.

Riley, M.A. (1978). Aging, social change, and the power of ideas. *Daedalus, 107* (4), 39–52.

Rinsley, D.B. (1977). An object-relations view of borderline personality. In P. Hartocolis (Ed.), *Borderline personality disorders* (pp. 47–70). New York: International Universities Press.

Rinsley, D.B. (1982). *Borderline and other self disorders: A developmental and object-relations perspective.* New York: Jason Aronson.

Sarwer-Forner, G.J. (1976). An approach to the global treatment of border-line patients: Psychoanalytic, psychotherapeutic, and psychopharmaco-logic considerations. In P. Hartocolis (Ed.), *Borderline personality disorders* (pp. 345–364). New York: International Universities Press.

Schafer, R. (1968). *Aspects of internalization.* New York: International Universities Press.

Silverman, L.H., Lachmann, F.M., & Millich, R.H. (1982). *The search for oneness.* New York: International Universities Press.

Takahashi, T. (1980). Adolescent symbiotic psychopathology. *Bulletin of the Menninger Clinic, 44* (3), 272–288.

Verney, T., & Kelly, J. (1981). *The secret life of the unborn child.* New York: Summit Books.

Woodger, J.H. (1952). *Biology and language.* Cambridge: Cambridge University Press.

3 The Membership Perspective of Social Work Practice

The conversion of human behavior concepts into principles that guide social workers who help clients is the logical next step in the explication of the membership perspective. This conversion is an analytic, and only secondarily an attitudinal, process.

While many think of social work as one social arrangement among many similar ones, the more predominant and more erroneous perception is that social work is so special and so esoteric that it shares little, if anything, with other helping professions or other aspects of human life. Careful analysis suggests, however, that social work is really a current expression of an old theme, one that is Biblical, indeed pre-Biblical, in origin. Tropp (1968) recognized this truth nearly 20 years ago. His point was that the group in social work practice has many similarities to all other groups and should be accorded, therefore, the respect of all who place value on human life. The membership perspective shares Tropp's view but modifies it in the sense that the respect Tropp refers to is accorded more to the members than to the group. This is not only because the members are social work clients, but because members constitute the human community, which is expressed in a myriad of small groups. The small group, in turn, is the seedbed, the great teacher, and the promoter of human membership. Thus, member, group, and community converge toward a unity that individualism cannot achieve.

The consistent point of reference in this chapter is the membership of client and social worker, who together have the task of finding solutions to problems of daily living. Only from this consistent vantage point can a relatively steady view of the many elements and aspects of the helping effort be obtained.

There is another reason for the adoption of the client–social worker focus. Too often, deliberations on major social policy questions fail to reflect the fact that sooner or later policy decisions are manifested in the lives of clients. The usual explanation is that legislation affecting thousands cannot address each member. But the truth is that the social worker, as an instrumentality through which the consequences of societal and community decisions are given meaning, does just that. The social worker and the client together deal with the possibilities and limitations inherent in social services, the nature of which is shaped by policies made by people with very different responsibilities from those of the social worker and client.

Thus, the social worker is not merely a mediator or even an intermediary between the client-member and the community. The social worker is an expression of society; but the social worker also has his or her own views and opinions. This fact often presents social workers with a painful dilemma and requires that they work within limitations they would rather avoid. This is particularly true when they are aware of the consequences and inadequacies of the piecemeal mosaic of social welfare planning, programming, and financing that constitutes the American social welfare system. The temptation to divest oneself of involvement always lies near. There are only two major alternatives. One is to work within the realm of the possible, and the other is to work for social change by linking those problems that arise in social worker–client relationships to those that arise in legislatures and administrative agencies. Whether the participants are social workers, legislators, administrators, voluntary givers, taxpayers, or clients, they all address essentially similar concerns and illustrate the fact that social welfare, whatever its quality, is a community concern.

This introduction serves as context for the discussion of the core of social work that follows. This core consists of five components: (1) a definition of social work practice; (2) the social work problem; (3) access to service—organizational and behavioral; (4) the membership group in social work; and (5) practice principles in social work.

THE CORE OF SOCIAL WORK

The core characteristics of social work capture the essence of what the profession is and what it tries to accomplish. This essence consists of the essential attributes of social work and mutes the similarities between social work and the cognate professions, as well as those aspects of the social work profession that are significant but relatively less determinative of social work's basic identity. The five central components noted above are descriptive of social work's essence because: (1) a social worker without a clear view of his or her profession cannot really function as a professional; (2) social work's role is and needs to be limited, as is the role of any other profession; (3) social work needs to consider how persons become clients and what skills and competencies are needed to be a client; (4) the client(s)–social worker relationship is indispensable to helping; and (5) social workers guide their activities across many client configurations and many problems.

Membership, by definition, narrows the distance between social worker and client. The guiding concept for the social worker–client relationship is mutuality. Mutuality means that whatever is done *for* the client is done *with* the client to the greatest possible extent.

A DEFINITION OF SOCIAL WORK PRACTICE

In Chapter 2, the two governing principles of constant connectedness and conditional accessibility were discussed. These two principles constitute the human behavioral basis for membership. Here, the membership concept is carried forward and utilized to redefine social work practice. Thus, *social work practice is to render professional aid in the management of membership.* The elements of this definition are further defined as follows:

Professional

The term professional encompasses the disciplined use of oneself (i.e., the use of valid knowledge, adequate insight, and self-control regarding the use of one's emotions in the social worker–client relationship). The disciplined use of knowledge is related to rational action, as well as to the discovery and application of new knowledge or developments.

Aid

The term aid refers to the social worker's role definition (i.e., to the activities in which the social worker engages). In sum, they are to help clients realize their resourcefulness as members of family and community, the workplace, and other groups. The social worker, as provider of aid, carefully observes his or her tendencies to do too much or too little.

The Management of Membership

Management refers to the purposeful use of one's competence and the assumption of responsibility for its use. The autonomy that is implicit in this formulation suggests ability to observe and make use of the behavior of other people, as well as one's own, in order to come to terms with and solve problems and difficulties in social living. Finally, management implies conscious action, the ability to make choices designed to improve the quality of membership with others.

THE SOCIAL WORK PROBLEM

Social workers are involved in a wide variety of personal and community issues. The question, however, is whether the distinctions between the personal and the public are as clear or as legitimate as they seem to be. This question has had to do with how problems are defined. Marital problems, for example, are defined in personal terms. A moment's thought, however, reveals that a great many others besides the partners are affected. Besides family and friends, for example, the social worker, to whom the partners turn for help with their marital problems, is a third person and a stranger.

Similarly, public issues are also personal ones because they affect many members. Policy issues that have to do with financing health care, for example, have immediate effects upon particular persons. *Private* and *public* are words that must be used with care, since what is private, or public, or both, is not easily definable, and certainly not in categorical terms.

A social problem becomes a social work problem when (1) there is a definable, potential client; (2) the client is able and ready to address his or her needs or difficulties; (3) there is a social worker available to render services; and (4) there is a reasonable expectation that the mutual efforts of social worker and client will succeed.

When a social problem becomes a social work problem, it is also a shared one. Professions are public institutions and in a very real way speak for the community. The fact that the social worker is bound by the ethics of confidentiality does not compromise this fact, since the obligation itself arises from professional practice and not from the agreement made each time the social worker and client decide to work together. The confidentiality ethic arises from the profession itself. It becomes reality in practice because the social worker, as a member of the profession, promises to abide by the profession's rules. It should be remembered, however, that confidentiality is constrained by legal requirements and weakened whenever more than one client is involved, none of whom owe each other secrecy unless they agree to do so voluntarily.

The conclusion is that social workers do all they can to protect their clients from harm. They recognize, nevertheless, that the promise of privacy is a tenuous one in practice, that concern for the client's welfare can only protect privacy to a degree, and that the sharing of social problems with others is, by its very nature, a less than private membership operation.

Access: The Social Agency and the Client

In order to determine who is eligible for services, social agencies apply admissions criteria and procedures. Potential clients must demonstrate that their condition or situation is amenable to the mission of the agency as defined either by legislation or a governing board. The documentation of eligibility for services or benefits usually takes place in an intake interview. This interview may be a formal one in an office, or informal and brief. The objective is to develop helping groups of eligible clients and social workers. Because these procedures are those of an organization, they are structural access mechanisms.

A second type of access mechanism is behavior, and it is associated with the competency required to act in the client role. While the client role is discussed in more detail in Chapter 4, it is necessary at this point to explain behavioral access mechanisms to emphasize the fact that how the social agency organizes itself to admit clients is not, by itself, a satisfactory definition of access. The client is not just a passive recipient of help. Indeed, the client is expected to be active, to be capable of working with a social worker. Such clients, however, cannot be taken for granted. There are, unfortunately, many potential clients who do not have these skills, and there are even some who may never acquire them. Membership can indeed be taken for granted as a basic human condition, but the ability to be a client cannot.

Table 3.1 illustrates the relationship of three elements of membership management in social work practice. The first column lists examples of client needs and problems typically encountered by social workers. These examples are illustrative, not exhaustive.

The second column addresses the membership characteristics discussed in Chapter 2. It will be noted that explicit mention of physical functioning has been omitted in the table. There are two reasons for this omission. First, physical functioning is universal to all people in all situations and therefore does not need special mention. Second, unless health issues are specifically known, social workers do not typically address them in practice. Even when known, the issue for social workers is one of understanding the impact of physical illness or disability on social, symbolic, and psychological functioning, rather than on the physical condition per se.

TABLE 3.1 Membership Management in Social Work Practice

Typical client needs and problems	Membership characteristics	Skills and access mechanisms
Adopting a child	Social functioning	Verbal application and consideration of implications
	Symbolization	Considering the meanings of adoption
	Internalization	Mother–child, father–child, couple–child relationships
Release from prison	Social functioning	Planning for the future, immediate and beyond
	Symbolization	Consideration of the meaning of having "a record"
	Internalization	Relations of self and others with the client as offender or felon
Marital difficulties	Social functioning	Showing distress, talking, discussion with spouse and social worker
	Symbolization	Attachment of meaning to troubles regarding identity as spouse and as man and woman
	Internalization	Failed marriage relationship
Raising funds	Social functioning	Working in group, i.e., committees, task forces, etc.
	Symbolization	Identification of meanings regarding work on behalf of others
	Internalization	Images of self and community

Cont.

TABLE 3.1 *Continued*

Typical client needs and problems	Membership characteristics	Skills and access mechanisms
Illness and injury	Social functioning	Verbal, emotional considerations of social concomitants of illness, injury, disability, i.e., financial, insurance, becoming well, accepting physical limitations
	Symbolization	The meaning of dependence on others The meaning of role changes as the result of impaired health, injury, or disability
	Internalization	The change from being "like other people" to images of being an ill, injured, or disabled member in one's own eyes and in the eyes of others

The third column lists skills and access mechanisms needed by clients to address the need or problem under consideration. When, for example, a child is being adopted, the adoptive parents need to consider what it means to adopt a child. It is also necessary to internalize a view of themselves and the child as belonging to one another. Or consider the case of a person about to be released from prison. The prisoner and his or her family need to consider the implications of his or her imminent release from prison and the implications of the prisoner's return to society in the immediate and long-range future. What will it mean, for example, to have a prison record, particularly for finding employment? What will be the nature of the relationships between the ex-prisoner, his or her family, and others? How will all of these matters be internalized? Will the picture rendered for the future be optimistic? Will it be realistic?

In considering the items in Column 3, two other points need to be made. First, if the client does not already have the skills listed in the column, they must be acquired. It is a mistake to assume that all the clients possess these skills. In many cases, they have to be taught if the client is to deal effectively with the problem or need at hand. Second, each skill is both a potential and actual access mechanism. *Access mechanism* in this case is defined as the exercise of the skill or skills needed to deal effectively with the need or problem. It cannot be taken for granted that clients know how to use social work services or that they know how to make creative use of their membership in a helping group. It cannot be assumed that they know how to explore the need or problem or how to discuss alternative ways of dealing with it. Indeed, clients may not know how to gain access to either the problem or to help with the problem.

THE HELPING GROUP IN SOCIAL WORK

The helping group is the most important core characteristic of social work practice. It overshadows all other considerations, whatever their significance might be, in the larger social welfare effort because at some point a social worker and one or more clients come together to work together. This coming together aims at the attainment of specific, agreed-upon goals. The planning, legislative enactments, administrative rules and procedures, fund-raising efforts, and other activities of thousands of other members (professionals, legislators, bureaucrats, volunteers, taxpayers, citizens) are the means that make the helping group possible.

The differences between those members who take advantage of the opportunity offered by the helping group to work on the resolution of their problems or the attainment of their needs, and those who make this opportunity possible, are not nearly as great or dramatic as is often thought. The "they" who are the clients of the "us" who make the policy decisions can easily be reversed. Similarly, clients and social workers can be both, given the right conditions and qualifications. While it is necessary to keep roles clearly defined, it is also true that the membership perspective makes it possible to see that whatever "side" one might be on, the work is by the community of which all are members and in which all have some kind of investment.

It is the membership dimension of the human condition, in the most general sense and in social work in particular, that clarifies the match of personal problem with public concern. Thus, the entire social welfare undertaking consists of community-based social services that are self-help devices that protect their own interests for the sake of a stable, predictable, just, and fair way of life. This does not in any way diminish the importance of each member. Rather, it makes it possible to understand how and why each member is important. This is because each member is, by definition, also an aspect of others.

Social work can represent each client as member. It can embrace the values of a society that recognizes the indivisibility of membership at all levels of social organization. It can work for an organized society that by definition respects each member and, therefore, all members.

Understanding the helping situation as a helping group brings further insights about membership with it. These insights have implications for the relationships between social values and science. For example, one manifestation of social work's traditional partiality toward individualism lies in its heavy emphasis on psychology. This stress on the mental life of people tends to introduce a sense of imbalance into the psychosocial equation that strongly favors the psychological. Hollis and Woods (1981) demonstrate this nearly exclusive preoccupation of some practitioners with the psychological while simultaneously acknowledging the importance of the social.

Furthermore, the social work helping group is more than just another interesting social arrangement. Social work is sanctioned and funded by society; it is one of society's agents of social control. Thus, the public tends to take the position that in return for public support, clients should act, and social workers should make them act, in ways the public thinks they should. Having recognized this, one comes to the conclusion that social work is not a profession free from undue outside influence. This is one of the painful yet realistic implications of the membership theme in social work. The society that creates, supports, and maintains social work, in whatever form and however inadequately, will have it no other way.

Finally, two faulty generalizations need to be taken into account before it is possible to speak intelligently of help-giving and help-taking. The first faulty generalization is the description of the unit of service in community social work. Since no one can work with a community, it is important to understand that community social work is work on behalf of the community through small groups that supposedly represent it. Nor is the matter clarified by distinctions between growth and task-oriented groups, or between so-called therapy groups serving the needs of individuals and task-oriented groups in the form of committees (Toseland & Rivas, 1984). In fact, distinctions are misleading. Indeed, the time when groups concerned with personal issues were open-ended, without stated purposes, is long past. Today, acceptable social work practice is widely defined in terms of objectives, measurable outcomes, and accountability on the part of the social worker (Fortune, 1985). From this standpoint, all helping efforts are task-oriented.

A second faulty generalization occurs when the individualism implicit in the term "therapy" (personal growth and problem solving) and the publicness of community work are dichotomized. When this occurs, the result is the isolation of the supposed individual. Similarly, the fact that members of committees also have personal needs that are regularly played out in committees and on boards is overlooked (Bakalinsky, 1984; Tropman, Johnson, & Tropman, 1979). Their needs generally go unattended by social workers who reply to questions about their practice in such situations with the comment: "I am not here to do therapy."

The Helping Group and Its Members

In the membership perspective, the helping group is defined as one or more clients and a social worker. That is, it consists of those who come into face-to-face interaction with a social worker, regardless of specific purpose, number, or composition of members. All that is needed is a social worker and at least one client. The goal may be personal assistance, or community organization, or planning, or the accomplishment of administrative tasks. Social work practice has to do with social situations in which members need to make decisions and initiate action, be they personal or on behalf of a community. The modality through which this all occurs is the helping group.

The activity of the social worker is called membership work. The necessary ingredients of this work are the existence of (1) social services; (2) professionally educated social workers; and (3) clients whose issues, problems, and needs are amenable to social work intervention and who possess the minimum skills required to participate in the work for which they come to the social agency and social worker. In all cases, the success of the membership work is determined by its relevance in the outside world. Thus, the work of client and social work members is to be measured from the beginning. Clients who do well in their helping group are either assumed to be doing well in their daily lives or, if they are not, the reasons for their not doing well need to be explained. Similarly, the committee member who does well in the group, but who fails to carry through on his or her responsibilities afterwards, is rendering no service to the potential beneficiaries in the community. In part, this evaluation occurs in the helping group itself through a variety of feedback behaviors by one or several other members. The final judgment, however, is available only when the consequences of the membership work are subjected to examination.

The Seen and the Unseen Group

When several people are observed interacting, they are referred to as a "seen" group. Thus, whether several clients see the social worker in an actual face-to-face group, or whether only one client comes to the social worker, the helping group is a seen group because the work is performed by those who are present and observable.

There is also, however, that world beyond those who are present and observable, that world beyond the seen group. This world consists of groups to which the client(s) belong that are not directly visible to members of the seen helping group. They are designated as "unseen groups" (Falck, 1981). It is in this world, beyond the seen group, that the work of the social worker and the client(s) is judged, primarily on the basis of the helping group's effect on the daily lives of client members.

Regardless of the size of any seen helping group, every client and social worker carries a myriad of previous experiences in groups. All members bring to the help group their unseen group memberships, namely, family, occupation, friends, church—all those meaningful others we all know about, even when they are not present. Thus, even when the only members of the helping group are one client and one social worker (the smallest "seen" group), their work is influenced by unseen groups. Indeed, the size of the helping group makes little difference. Unseen groups must always be attended to in any social work helping group, regardless of its size.

Unseen group influences in the helping group can be viewed from two perspectives. On the one hand, those who constitute the client's unseen groups are influenced by the work done in the helping group. On the other hand, those others who constitute the client's unseen groups can be viewed as active participants in the helping group because they influence from afar what occurs in the helping group. The client's unseen groups are not passive participants. They are active in their own ways. Thus, the social worker must bear in mind not only the seen group with which he or she is working, but multiple unseen groups as well. Their significance lies in the fact that it is the client who belongs to them, influences them, and, in turn, is influenced by them.

Seen and unseen groups have several implications that must be taken into account in social work helping groups. The first implication derives from recognition of the fact that all clients live in groups. This is what is meant by the word social. Consequently, the social worker focuses on the major reality of the client, that is, the client's behavior vis-á-vis other people. This does not mean that the social worker and client member must always talk about the client's unseen group life. It does mean, however, that the social worker always starts with the client's social reality, those aspects of the client's other group memberships that the client brings into the helping group and distills into behaviors that are immediately present.

The second implication is that all clients demonstrate their group life by (1) reporting it; (2) reenacting it; and (3) planning for it. These behaviors will be explored more fully in Chapter 4. At this point, however, it should be noted that the future to be planned is always in some social (group) situation to come. In the two-member helping group, the social worker helps the client project into the future in the planning process. In the larger helping group, the social worker and the clients are involved in experiences similar to the experiences of clients outside of the helping group. Thus, in larger helping groups, client behaviors can be seen *in natura*. It is this *in natura* situation that makes so much more readily apparent what it is that clients are going through in the world beyond the helping group. In summary, the now always gives rise to what is coming. Since the present foreshadows the future, it always presupposes some kind of planning in the helping group, some kind of projection toward some kind of behavior that is more satisfactory to the client than that of the past or present.

The third implication is that in helping groups, members are immediately accountable for their behavior. In the two-member helping group, this accountability occurs as the social worker and the client evaluate the effectiveness of what the client member is doing in the present situation and what the client member is experiencing in his or her life beyond the helping situation. In larger helping groups, members are immediately accountable for their behavior to one another because the other client members are present. It is the genius and the nature of the group that there is no real postponement of the effects of member behavior on others. In groups, members tend to react immediately, visibly, and sometimes loudly. This reaction may be one of silence, but it usually consists of words that are formulated in certain ways and spoken in certain tones that let each member, including the social worker, know at all times who stands how with whom. This accountability, and the evaluation implicit in it, lies at the core of group life.

Psychosociological Levels of Groups

Viewing groups from a psychosociological perspective complements the seen and unseen perspective of groups. This enlarged understanding of groups brings different kinds of groups into a rational relationship with one another and makes it possible to distinguish one type from another.

In this connection, the question of the psychosocial proximity of members is of relevance in defining who is and who is not a member of any given social situation, such as a family, a community, an occupational group, an institution. The greater the psychosocial distance between members, the less intimate the relationships are among them. The less face-to-face contact among members, the less personal the perceptions of each other and the more impersonal the decision making on matters affecting the fate and future of people. The legislator who passes, or declines to pass, social legislation affecting people never seen, for example, is in a different position from the social worker who makes home visits to people who live in physical misery as a result of social policy limitations or the absence of relevant social policy.

When the matter is examined from the standpoint of professional social work, it is possible to conceptualize three types of groups, namely the primary, the secondary, and the tertiary group. Each has its own characteristics and possibilities in social work practice. As consideration of each type makes clear, the term *helping* is more directly applicable to the first two types than it is to the third.

The Primary Group

The primary group is distinguished by the fact that its members interact in face-to-face situations and their relationships are of an intimate nature. The most obvious examples of the primary group are families and close friendships. If the qualities of the primary group relationship are positive, the helping nature of the group derives from its composition and interaction. If the relationship qualities are negative, the primary group may still become a helping group with the help of a social worker who identifies and builds on the member strengths found in the family to resolve problems and promote positive social functioning.

The Secondary Group

The secondary group is defined by the nonintimate nature of its relationship and by the fact that interaction is face-to-face. Examples of secondary groups include co-workers, club members, church members, neighbors, and others with whom one interacts face-to-face but with whom one's relationship is nonintimate in the affective sense. It is the variable of affective intimacy that distinguishes the primary from the secondary group, as comparison of a family and office mates, for example, makes readily apparent.

Thus, the interaction of a social worker and several nonrelated clients satisfies the definition of the secondary group as a helping group, as does the interaction of one client and a social worker. The fact that in time relationships of considerable depth and importance may develop in a secondary helping group does not, in and of itself, change the fact that it is a secondary rather than a primary group.

The distinction between primary and secondary groups remains, despite the depth of the helping group's relationships.

The Tertiary Group

The tertiary group is describable by the fact that it involves a non-face-to-face and nonintimate situation. Examples of tertiary groups include citizenship, government, socioeconomic class, affiliation with institutional religions, cultural and language groups, race, political parties, professional associations, and other regional, national, or international groups of people with whom one does not have face-to-face contact.

Strictly speaking, it is difficult to think of such groups as helping groups because their members do not see one another. It is the mechanism of representation that reduces most such groups to the point where they can be dealt with in reality terms. One example of a tertiary group is the community, but the community becomes a helping group only when representatives of the community meet to address community problems. This phenomenon will be accorded more attention in Chapter 6. At this point, it is important to bear in mind the distinctions between tertiary groups and the other two types of groups. These distinctions are summarized in Table 3.2.

The conceptualization of types of groups as primary, secondary, and tertiary differs somewhat from traditional conceptualizations in three ways. First, the notion of the helping group (or helping situation) is not conceptualized only in terms of the face-to-face interactions of social worker and clients, as the concept of the tertiary group illustrates. The concept of the unseen group, discussed above, also illustrates this fact.

TABLE 3.2 Characteristics of Helping Groups

Type of group	Face-to-face interaction	Intimacy
Primary	Yes	Yes
Secondary	Yes	No
Tertiary	No	No

A second difference is the definition of the social worker–client relationship as a group situation, that is, a helping group. Given the fact that social work has traditionally made a distinction between work with individuals and work with groups, this conceptual difference is a significant one. While social casework was defined as work with the individual, social group work was defined as work with the group on behalf of the individual. This point was discussed in Chapter 1. The membership perspective does not make such distinctions.

Third, the membership formulation reflects the human condition. As a consequence it evolves not as an integration or combination of traditional social work methods, but rather from a new synthesis of human behavior building blocks. It is the concept of membership that combines the individual, group, and community into this new synthesis, undergirded by the twin principles of constant connectedness and conditional accessibility. This also explains why the dyad, consisting of the social worker and one client, is regarded as the smallest helping group. It follows, therefore, that the social worker is a member, in principle, like any other human being who interacts, with the difference located in the role he or she plays, not in whether or not the social worker is a member.

THE UNIVERSALITY OF MEMBERSHIP IN SOCIAL WORK

The membership perspective in social work holds that the basic unit of service is the member in the community. The number of people present in any one group is of less importance than awareness that this definition of the unit of service has consequences for practice. The fact that one is a member means that people share a common experience, a history that is ineradicable. Each time it occurs, membership rearticulates the beginnings of life and its interactional processes, even as early as intrauterine life itself. At this level of consideration, the *fact* of membership precedes the *kind* of membership, that is, the roles one takes on in human interaction. Similarly, the role of the social worker rests on the basic membership role of the professional. The control needed to assure that the work is done properly is the intellectual and emotional self-discipline the professional brings to the helping situation.

One manifestation of their professional knowledge and self-discipline has to do with the manner in which social workers help clients make decisions. It is also apparent in their views about the rights of clients, society, and the social worker.

The conceptual, and by implication the philosophical, justification for self-determination in traditional formulations of social work were reviewed in Chapter 1. Here the argument is carried a step further to expand upon the meaning of decision making when viewed from the membership perspective. To put it simply, one of the inescapable consequences of using the right to self-determination as the philosophical rationale for decision making is that one either encourages clients to think only of their own interests or to think of themselves as the sole person who determines what to do and what not to do. While it is, indeed, possible to "do one's own thing" without conscious regard for its effects upon others, and while one may also hold that behavior is always personal, in the membership perspective the who and how of decision making in social work is determined by the answers to questions about the definition of clientship. Should the answer be that the client is an individual, the consequent effect is clear—decisions are made by individuals for individuals. Should the answer be that the client is a member, the consequences are equally clear, since the membership perspective holds that all behavior affects those who engage in it. Thus, decision making rests on social self-determination. The term social refers to the social nature of each human being (and client or social worker) and, at the same time, to the fact that no matter what the decision, there are consequences with which not only the decision maker but also others must live.

It is relatively easy to see that a person who makes decisions lives with his or her consequences and is responsible for them. This is sometimes less clear when trying to visualize the effects of one person's decision on others. There are two reasons why this is so. The first addresses the effects of behavior. Those who live in the same house and interact, for example, are usually those most aware of the actions of the others who live in the house. This awareness is at the heart of social work situations where members see and hear what any one of them does and react in their own ways. The second reason is that the effect occurs in the realm of meanings. That is, the client who makes decisions communicates not only the behavior attending each decision and the decision itself, but also triggers interpretations of the decision in others. This interpretation, called symbolization, or the assignment of meaning to behavior, extends far beyond the face-to-face group. A great many clients never come, or need to come, into contact with those who are affected by them. The youth gang member, for example, rarely faces those he damages. Similarly, the beneficiaries of community-wide fund-raising efforts do not usually know those who made possible the services they provide or use. Moreover, the meanings assigned to decisions about which services these funds will be used to support can range from hurt, damage, and destruction on the one hand to benefit, opportunity, and satisfaction on the other.

If the membership perspective contains one prescription for social work practice, it is that all decision making in which the social worker has any involvement must take into account the client and the meanings the client's decisions have for other people. The degree to which "one's thing" is "one's own" is governed by the irreducible fact of membership.

One could argue this point from the standpoint of morality, as Siporin (1982) has done. The question to be answered is whether social work can be an "amoral" profession and at the same time fulfill its social mandate. Siporin does not think so. The argument that the social worker is also a member, not an outside observer of what happens in the social work helping group, supports this position. Yet the case made here rests less on considerations of morality or amorality in social work than it does on the implications and demands of the irreducible membership of all people. Thus, freedom is social freedom, self-determination is social self-determination (decision making by the social self), and the social worker's role is one of holding up to clients the irreducible nature of one's sociality. The universality of membership applies in social work as it does everywhere else. What distinguishes social work is its ability to focus on this universality in a set of ideas that give it its mission and its credibility.

SOCIAL WORK PRACTICE PRINCIPLES
IN THE MEMBERSHIP PERSPECTIVE

The final item among the core characteristics of social work is a set of practice principles that emanate from the membership perspective. "Practice principles prescribe what a practitioner should do in a given situation" (Blythe & Briar, 1987, p. 495). Practice principles, therefore, are the dimensions a practitioner keeps in mind during and between contact with clients; they explain how the social worker might understand the nature of the relationship between and among them and, most of all, the nature of the required interventions.

An example of a practice principle is that the conscious use of self is to be identified and monitored in social work interventions. In return for the privilege of helping others, the professional is obligated to handle himself or herself in a self-disciplined way. Ethically, self-discipline protects the client and the social worker, especially on the emotional, often unconscious level, where the influences of clients and the social worker contribute to each other as well as take their toll on one another. The management of countertransference is one of the great and steady challenges to all in the helping professions, including social work (Hollis & Woods, 1981, pp. 293–295).

The main advantage of practice principles is to be found in the fact that their clarity enables one to guide one's work consistently. At the same time, to be effective, practice principles allow for flexibility and for self-correction when their strengths and weaknesses become clear in practice.

Seven practice principles that derive from the membership perspective are capable of helping practitioners understand what they see and hear from their clients. In addition, they point toward intervention. These seven practice principles are:

1. *The behavior of clients is to be understood as membership behavior.* Reports by clients of experience with others, past, present, and anticipated in the future, are to be viewed as expressions of their social characteristics.

2. *The social worker's interventions in the presence of clients or on their behalf are to be understood as membership behaviors.* To view the social worker as a member makes no statement other than what may be said about clients. The differences lie in the kinds of memberships, not in their definition. The social worker plays a professional role that is consistent with all other membership requirements and in addition defines that role so as to perform certain functions that are not performed by people who are not social workers.

3. *Statements by members of the helping group are to be treated as statements about the speaker and either those others to whom they are directed and/or others in the members' lives who are not present.* It is implicit in the membership perspective that if everyone is a member, everyone affects everyone else. The concept of social reciprocity underlines this idea, that is, that a member's basic sociality derives from the interactions of self and others.

4. *Personality dynamics in the membership perspective are to be understood as derivative of the interaction of the biological and the social aspects of the member.* Most characteristic of the human member is the interplay between biological and social substrates that produces personality. Personality characteristics are private mental phenomena. In practical terms, personality may be inferred from the particular, if not unique, ways in which a given member conducts his or her membership behaviors.

5. *The client's rights and obligations concerning decision making are to be viewed as manifestations of social self-determination.* The "social" in "social self-determination" denotes the fact that in origin and in consequence, behavior is social.

6. *Helping situations are to be viewed in terms of group membership.* The membership perspective does not describe group behavior but instead focuses on the behavior of members in the group. Groups cannot behave, only members can. The members may number two or more, that is, the social worker and one or more clients.

7. *Social work intervention is to be linked to only those purposes that account for the fact that the social worker and client members work together.* This practice principle takes us back to an earlier stage in the discussion about the core characteristics of professional social workers. These core characteristics are: (1) the ability to use the intellect, (2) to be self-directed in the use of data whether they come from clients, the literature, or research, and (3) skill in use of emotional discipline coupled with emotional availability to clients.

PRELIMINARY OBSERVATIONS
ABOUT PRACTICE METHODOLOGY

Given these observations, the following generalization is offered: *Those needs and problems that are understandable and definable in membership terms are the province of social work intervention. Those not definable in these terms are beyond the purview of the social worker and should, therefore, be the responsibility of others to address.* Illness, for example, is not a membership issue, but the social concomitants of illness are. Physicians, therefore, treat the one, while social workers legitimately address the other. The legal consequences of committing a crime are not issues of membership, but the social consequences are, as they affect both the family of the offender and the victims of the crime. Hence, the social worker becomes involved with the accused or convicted member and his or her family and others whose future is, in large part, determined by the accused.

We thus return to the helping group and think of it as a configuration of members (including the social worker member) who help each other or at least affect each other. The overall aim is the evaluation and revision of membership behavior as guided by clearly stated purposes. In these helping groups, the self and the other are viewed in terms of continuities and semipermeable boundaries. The concept of the social work helping group rests on the fact of membership. Thus, it is that the very method employed by social workers is thought of and referred to as the membership method.

Nomenclature is significant because it indicates what theorists and methodologists consider to be of importance. This, in turn, impacts on practitioners, who conceptualize themselves, their clients, and their methodologies to fit their objectives. Since the aim of social work is to render aid in the management of membership, the method employed to pursue this objective is the membership method. The goals to be accounted for and to be evaluated are stated in behavioral terms because membership translates into membership behavior, that is, action. It follows, therefore, that the principles that undergird membership practice need to be stated in similar terms.

This emphasis in no way underplays the psychological aspects of personality-influenced behavior. With the unit of intervention defined as the member or members among members, personality theory—in this case psychoanalytic object-relations theory—is employed as the means to understand the member in social interaction.

CONCLUSION

The purpose of this chapter was to present the core elements of the membership perspective of social work: (1) the definition of social work; (2) the social work problem; (3) access to service; (4) the helping group in social work; and (5) practice principles in social work. The universality of the membership perspective and preliminary observations about practice methodology were also considered. These core components combine to produce a cohesive and understandable approach, applicable to many varieties of social work practice.

The two principles of membership behavior, constant connectedness and conditional accessibility, remain intact and are implicit not only in the chapter just ended but also as we continue on to the discussion of the client as member. It should be kept in mind that membership is a condition of being human, with all its implications that compel our attention.

REFERENCES

Bakalinksy, R. (1984). The small group in community organization practice. *Social Work with Groups, 7* (2), 87–96.
Blythe, B.J., & Briar, S. (1987). Direct practice effectiveness. In A. Minahan (Ed.-in-chief), *Encyclopedia of social work* (18th ed.) (Vol. I, pp. 399–407). Silver Spring, MD: National Association of Social Workers.

Falck, H.S. (1981). *The "seen" and the "unseen" group in clinical social work practice.* Monograph #3 in the health social work practice series. Richmond, VA: Virginia Organization of Health Care Social Workers.

Fortune, A.E. (Ed.). (1985). *Task-centered practice with families and groups.* New York: Springer Publishing Company.

Hollis, F., & Woods, M.E. (1981). *Social casework: A psychosocial therapy* (3rd ed.). New York: Random House.

Siporin, M. (1982). Moral philosophy in social work today. *Social Service Review, 56* (4), 516–538.

Toseland, R.W., & Rivas, R.F. (1984). *An introduction to group work practice.* New York: Macmillan.

Tropp, E. (1968). The group: In life and in social work. *Social Casework, 5,* 267–274.

Tropman, J., Johnson, H., & Tropman, E. (1979). *The essentials of committee management.* Chicago: Nelson Hall.

4 The Client as Member

In this chapter, attention shifts to the role of clients in social work helping groups. As already noted, the definition of *client* has major implications for social work theory and practice. The definition of client in the membership perspective is substantially different from its traditional formulations. Tropp (1974), one of the few social work theorists to glimpse the potential implications of the membership concept, was well aware of the importance of such matters. In his trenchant discussion of key social work terms, he concluded:

> [T]his. . .membership concept, if applied to the multiplicity of existing social services, may appear to represent a wrenching, threatening reshifting of relations between user and provider. If it does threaten, then something is truly out of kilter between what exists and what social workers keep claiming to represent: the democratic ethos, mutuality, and open agreements openly kept. It is only a wrench for those who have not been doing business in this way. (p. 29)

THE PRINCIPLES OF CLIENTSHIP

When seen through the lens of membership, "self-help" becomes "social self-help" and is governed by four principles that apply equally to clients and social workers. These are (1) the simultaneity of self and other; (2) the reciprocity of "we" and "I"; (3) the definition of freedom as social product; and (4) decision making as social self-determination.

The principle of the simultaneity of self and other denotes the fact that all human action, with the exception of certain biological givens, is social interaction to which meaning is assigned. The principle of the reciprocity of "we" and "I" suggests that the basis of human reality is the human group and community. Furthermore, given the semipermeability of boundaries, all aspects of human life constitute a seamless continuity. Any newly born person, for example, is simultaneously a product of a "we" and a social contributor to that "we."

The third and fourth principles are implied in the first two and derive from them. The definition of freedom as a social product is not only empirically observable, it is also common sense. If, for example, the individual did, in fact, exist in nature, there could be no concept of freedom since there would be no one else to be free from. It is because people are members and do, in fact, exist in groups that freedom has meaning. Freedom is a social quality, not an individual one. Its existence or absence is a social product. Decision making, therefore, is a social process and hence it has a close link to social self-determination.

CLIENTSHIP AS SELF-HELP

Being a client is to be in a self-help role. There are two essential elements of this role: (1) recognition that one needs, or ought to accept, help; and (2) those actions that enable the client to take and use help productively. Clientship is expressed in two interlocked ways that articulate social cause and social consequence. This is so not only because the persons involved in the process are social by definition, but also because the process involves a social worker who, acting on behalf of the client and engaged by him or her, evokes and represents a wider concern, that is, society. Social maladaption, social dysfunction, and personal difficulty are clearly matters of social interest.

The self-help aspects of clientship are, as a consequence, those that help society (the tertiary group), and it is this fact that places the social agency and the social worker in a self-help stance. This is so even when the help given and received is personal in nature. Clientship is also a self-help role because it is as a member that the client helps himself or herself. When he or she is successful, the other membership groups to which he or she belongs also benefit. Similarly, in helping clients, social workers also help, or act in their own interests and causes, because they also affect other members, such as the client's unseen groups, personnel in the social agency, other social workers, and the community.

To achieve such outcomes, the social worker and client(s) form a helping group that mirrors the client's behavior elsewhere in unseen groups and makes it possible for the social worker, and often for other clients as well, to understand how the client acts and how the client's actions (behavior) may have led him or her to seek help. This is not always the case, however, since all of the problems a client brings to the helping group are by no means a result of something dysfunctional the client did. Whether or not the helping group is used as a prototype, the primary emphasis in helping groups that address client needs is always the client as member of other, often unseen groups. For the client, the stage of action is daily life. It is from this vantage point that the work done in the helping group takes its specificity.

Relationship in Social Work Tradition

A most complicated task faced by social work is to treat the client as something other than just a case, a mechanical, neutral object of interest to the professionals involved (Perlman, 1979; Robinson, 1930). Because social workers have long recognized and valued the essential humanness of each client, they have given emphasis to process, to relationship, to the active involvement of the client at each and every stage of receiving help. No social work theorist has ever suggested that the client not be involved, or that it is the function and the right of the social worker to decide what is good for the client.

Concepts that illustrate the mainstream attitudes regarding relationship in social work practice include the following: "starting where the client is"; "moving only as the client is ready to move"; "assisting the client in his or her empowerment" (this being a recent prescription in social work theory); and emphasis on "the here and now." All of these injunctions have a fundamental ring to them. Yet it is not always easy to be explicit about what they mean, as the injunction to stay with "the here and now" illustrates. It is, after all, patently impossible not to stay with "the here and now," even when the conversational content has to do with the past.

At a minimum, so tradition holds, the social worker and the client have to get to know something about each other, to explore the meaning of being a client and of coming for help, as well as develop a modicum of trust. Such relationships are never merely to be established, but to be developed. Relationship implies time and process. At a maximum, and particularly in mental health agencies where some of the work to be done requires long-term intervention, the social worker looks for the ability of clients to form transferential relationships with the worker, the nature and depth of which allow more or less intensive exploration of personality-focused issues. Most social workers seek working relationships with their clients that permit doing whatever needs to be done in an atmosphere of relative openness and mutual involvement.

If this has been the tradition in social work, recent developments have modified it and need to be taken into account. Relatively recent changes in social work thought, for example, have brought into question the need for a relationship between social worker and client, as well as between clients themselves when the work takes place in groups larger than the dyad. Besides questioning a basic social work tradition, these changes also tend to promote a type of individualism that needs to be discarded rather than reinforced.

Recent Concepts of Relationship in Social Work

Few would argue that long-term intervention is necessarily better than short-term intervention, or vice versa. The issue is not length of intervention, but need. Ironically, the rise of modern short-term intervention, while without doubt of use to many clients, has introduced into the profession a sense of efficiency it never articulated before. There is an emphasis on the mutually arrived at contract, but this emphasis is tempered by the not-so-subtle suggestion that less time, rather than more, is better. Most social workers allow for a certain amount of prolongation of service in order to take unanticipated developments into account as the work gets under way. Contracts may range from 1 to 12 sessions. All involved can generally make reasonable predictions about the end of services. One is never quite sure, however, whether time is linked to need, to cost, or to social worker tolerance for long-term relationships.

Success or failure is determined by the type of assessment made, especially at the outset. The more behaviorally focused, the better the opportunity to see whether or not the client's behavior has changed as a result of social work intervention. When, for example, the assessment leads to an agreement that client and social worker will work on being assertive with one's spouse, the evidence of positive change is that the client speaks up when this is needed.

On the other hand, if the assessment leads to the observation that this client involves himself or herself repeatedly, and over long periods of time, in dependent relationships that are personally harmful, and that even now with awareness continues to do so, the interventions are both longer and more complex. Should it turn out, for example, that a male client has no problems finding work, because he has a marketable skill that pays well, but cannot hold a job for more than 3 months, something may be needed other than training him to hold his temper when he is criticized. The point is that long-term social services are less available than before. The elements that characterized them, such as emphasis on time, process, and relationship, are largely muted, if not abandoned. It is with this in mind that one must understand present perceptions of clients.

Associated with short-term and task models are such terms as accountability, service delivery, and cost-effectiveness. While the rhetoric of relationship remains untouched in these models, its reality has been substantially modified by these newer approaches. It is impossible, for example, to have much of a relationship with a hospitalized client for whom hospital discharge "planning" is restricted to 3 hours or less. One is skeptical when confronted by the assertion that relationship is replaceable or that it can be shortened to the point of disappearance. That skepticism rests on the impression that the motivation behind such assertions is often not *better* service in a short time, but *less* service for less money. There is the ever-present suspicion that to give more, rather than less, costs too much and presents the taxpayer and private donor with a bill they would rather not pay. However one argues the case, the impression persists that the totality of attitudes, and often the unspoken intent behind these changes, adds up to something other than the social work ideals implicit in the concept of a relationship with a trusted social worker who takes time to involve both clients and himself or herself in the rendering of aid, rather than simply "delivering service."

Were one to identify the major shortcoming and "cost" of short-term, task-oriented social work models at another level, it would surely be that they are concerned only marginally, if at all, with the client's membership outside the helping group. It is not that relatives and others are totally ignored, but that major, if not sole, attention is placed on the client's behaviors in *the present,* that is, in the helping group. There is no time or interest in considering thoughtfully and carefully what the changes the client seeks, or the decisions that are made, mean to others and, therefore, to the client as member of others. In this sense, short-term, task-oriented intervention encounters the same criticism that long-term psychoanalytically based social work efforts of the past encountered. In both cases, membership is overlooked because the unit of service is the individual and all others are "the environment."

Relationship in the Membership Perspective

Carlton (1984) defines relationship in social work as the connection and quality of clinical membership (p. 64). He points out that relationship lies at the heart of social work, and he documents this statement by reference to major theorists writing at different stages of social work's development as a profession. He cites Biesteck (1957) for his penetrating analysis of relationship. Although Biesteck defined relationship in individual terms, Carlton defines relationship in terms of membership:

> In the first sense, the sense of being related or being connected, relationship is synonymous with membership. As the social worker and the client(s) gain clinical membership, they become related, significant to one another, connected. . . .In the second sense, relationship

denotes the quality of the connection of the clinical social worker and the client(s). (pp. 66–67)

TIME DIMENSIONS IN
THE MEMBERSHIP PERSPECTIVE

The client in the role of self-helper attends, together with the social worker, to his or her tasks. Essentially three functions reside in this role, each of which is linked to a time-defined stage. The first of these functions is reporting. The second is reenaction, and the third is planning (Falck, 1981). These three functions illustrate the membership perspective in that they do not depend on absolute boundaries between an individual client and other individuals. Instead, they depend upon the definition of the person in consonance with membership. Neither reporting nor reenacting, with their overtones of transference, can rest on the closed boundaries of individuals. Furthermore, the viability of all three depend on the real or remembered presence of others.

The Client as Reporter

All clients are reporters. Through oral explication or other forms of behavioral report, they bring the experiences of their pasts and presents to the social worker and others. This is what is expected as the social worker encourages clients to report who they are, what they think and feel, what their dreams, hopes, and sometimes fantasies are, and how they see the world and themselves in it. As the social worker helps the client to report who he or she is, both the social worker's theoretical approach and, more importantly, the client's view of self can often be discerned. One way or another, the client reports, sometimes in very graphic ways, what his or her problems and concerns are and why he or she seeks help. Many people feel self-conscious about how their report makes them look in the eyes of others, including the social worker. And they tend to modify their reports in ways that seem logical as well as emotionally acceptable to the reporter. The picture that emerges from these reports may be positive or negative, or both. In any event, most clients put some investment into the manner in which they interpret the experiences of their past and present lives to others. They do this in words and other behavior. In short, they attempt to gain and maintain control over what they communicate and how they and others evaluate what they say. Those who come with great difficulty and those whose ability to seek assistance is relatively easy to observe render a picture of themselves that offers protection, avoids undue pain, and frequently overlooks what seems too hard to live with consciously. Yet the central point in reporting is that persons portray themselves not only in terms of the past moment reported, but also in terms of their present, somewhat selective memory of what preceded and followed it.

Thus, the client, as reporter, represents aspects of his or her experience in the form of stories about the past, as he or she remembers and interprets them in the present. The following vignette illustrates this point.

> CLIENT: I came here because I can't get along with anybody at home. My wife and the children and I have been fighting with each other for years. You can't know what my life is like or what it's been like for the last 10 years— nothing but fighting and yelling. It started right after my wife and I were married and it continued after the children came along. All I can remember is that when anybody wants anything, they yell.
>
> SOCIAL WORKER: And you?
>
> CLIENT: I always hid when my parents screamed at each other. I guess that's how I learned to protect myself.

Although this excerpt is a brief one, it is truly a report of a series of events (10 years of family life under painful conditions) that the client combines with a degree of insight ("I always hid. . . . [T]hat's how I learned to protect myself."). The client's comments about his parents have little in them that is accusatory.

The particular content of this self-report is less important than the fact that it illustrates the kind of communication that lays the basis for the common work of the helping group in such a way that the initial membership of the client and social worker can later be expanded to include the client's family members. Even when they are not physically present, however, the meaning of these family members to the client and the client's meaning to them is implicit in the client's report. It should also be noted that the client elaborates on his story by the way he speaks of the intensity of his feelings ("You can't know what my life is like or what it's been like. . . .").

In reporting and elaborating on facts, clients provide indications of how they manage their memberships. The client as reporter acts as a recorder of events and their interpretation. This record and interpretation are shared with the social worker.

The Client as Reenactor

The second function inherent in the client role is that of reenactor. By reenaction, clients project upon those present some of the qualities that they perceived in their relationship with others prior to the social work situation. People "find" people in the present situation who in some way remind them of the meanings of earlier experiences. Most of this is unconscious. Occasionally, the client is aware of this or may be made aware of it by the social worker. In general, however, reenactment is and remains unconscious.

In the continuation of the story begun in the vignette presented above, it is possible to discern the phenomenon of transference in the client's reenactment of his past relationships in his present situation.

CLIENT: I think a lot now about the constant screaming and how I can put an end to it. I know that I have something to do with it, but I don't know what. I have been coming here for 3 months now and you still haven't done anything to help me. [With his voice rising] I demand that you do something to get me out of this mess.

SOCIAL WORKER: You are yelling.

CLIENT: I've got to get out of this. I can't stand it. [The client shouts] Why can't anybody ever do what I want? Why do I always have to give in?

SOCIAL WORKER: You did not hear what I said. Perhaps you can see that you want me to yell at you. You become frustrated because I behave the way I do, rather than the way you want me to behave.

CLIENT: What? Oh, maybe you are right.

In this case, the client is more than the victim of what happens in the family. By participating in the yelling and shouting, by participating in the family's fights, he constantly reenacts his past in the present, as do the other family members. At the same time reenactment is not the same thing as simple repetition because over the years the actors have changed. The client's parents are no longer in the picture, but their roles have been assumed by the client's spouse and children, with the cooperation and participation of the client. The client has endowed his wife and children with the roles of his parents, thereby reenacting his childhood relationships.

The characteristics of the multiple-client helping groups are significant in this regard. The mutual confrontation that clients engage in, when they understand that a given member behaves repeatedly in ways "designed" to bring him or her harm, is a powerful tool for bringing about change. There is greater clarity not only about the fact that one constantly reenacts harmful behaviors, but also that peers disapprove of such behavior and let that be known. Conversely, clients in such situations have the opportunity to pick, as it were, certain, but not all, co-clients onto whom they project former relations with others. They do this by engaging in behaviors that are clearly transferential in nature. For many clients, this is a significant way of "using" other members to obtain help. One example is the young male client who picks a middle-aged woman onto whom he discharges a great deal of anger, if not hate, for reasons that have nothing to do with that person. Conversely, there is the young woman who protects an elderly male client who has neither asked for nor indicated the need for such solicitude. A third example is the teenager who eroticizes relationships with a co-client of the opposite sex without any indication that this is wanted by the co-client. If such a relationship is repeatedly turned down by the co-client, the client may even increase his or her erotically suggestive behavior. The point is that the availability to objects transference is never confined to the social worker alone. It can include all others in the helping group. And, since transference-based behavior has repetitive aspects, it is also reenactive.

The Client as Planner

The third function of the client role of self-helper, both in the multimember group and in a dyad, is that of planning. Perlman (1957) defines social work as problem solving within a relationship between a social worker and client(s). The logic of problem solving includes planning. It includes an assessment of the present and the desirable future and how that future might be realized.

Strictly speaking, planning is any activity that delineates action toward a specific goal and includes a convincing statement about its implementation. Effective planning always suggests either the participation of those affected by the plan or consideration of the others who may benefit or be harmed by it. In this sense, all planning is social planning, regardless of subject matter, the actor(s), or the probability of consequences.

The way planning is defined, however, can pose certain dangers for the outcome of the helping situation. Planning is overinclusive, for example, when any and all statements about future behavior are included in it. In such cases, such statements are better defined as vaguely formulated wishes. Seemingly vague plans by very ill people, however, may also pose dangers to others that need to be taken into account. On the other hand, planning can be defined too narrowly; that is, it can be underinclusive. One example of underinclusive planning is the rationally thought out plan that emphasizes the advantages it offers a particular person and overlooks the threat it poses to absent others, in other words, the client's absent groups.

One plans because there is hope in the world and because human beings are able to influence their memberships, both those that are within reach and those that are remote. The hope is that a better life lies within reach. It is this hope and this ability that encourages both the helper and the helped to engage in the arduous processes planning requires if it is to lead to positive change. Even if goals are never fully reached, most people are sufficiently bolstered by partial successes to keep hoping, working, and planning. This is the rationale for staying with the mutual process of rendering and using help. Without these beliefs, there would be little justification for what social workers and clients do together.

The quality of planning in the helping group is anticipatory in nature. It occurs each time the client asks for help, however indirectly, and indicates what he or she expects from it. This does not place the burden on the social worker alone, but includes what the client plans to do about the problem. This point is apparent in the continuation of the case vignette that follows.

> CLIENT: I am beginning to learn that not everyone yells when they are frustrated or want something. I have to let that sink in.
>
> SOCIAL WORKER: What do you mean?
>
> CLIENT: I'm so used to being yelled at and shouting back. I guess I just thought that was the way it had to be without ever really thinking about it, if you know what I mean.
>
> SOCIAL WORKER: I do, but now that you are thinking about it, what do you plan to do about it?
>
> CLIENT: I want to make some changes in the way I act. And I hope that everyone else in the house will too. I think it will get better if we all realize what we've been doing and try to do something about it.

In the client's movement toward a more clearly defined plan, it is possible to glimpse in this vignette his recognition of the problem, his part in it, and his sense of hope that he, and the others in his family, can do something about the way they interact that will make their life *together* better. In addition, this vignette illustrates the client as planner who, with his social worker, begins methodically to solve problems posed by very specific, concrete issues.

THE DIMENSIONS OF CLIENTSHIP

The client as reporter, reenactor, and planner implies the behaviors and interests of others who are not directly involved in the helping group. They are significant because of the role(s) they play in the genesis of the problems with which the client(s) struggles and also because they are involved in the resolution of these problems. Sometimes the involvement of these significant others is direct; sometimes it is indirect. Sometimes they are involved knowingly; often they are without awareness of their involvement. These significant others constitute the client's seen and unseen group members. In social work, one observation about seen and unseen groups stands out above all others. It is that in every aspect of clientship, while those present are of importance, the more lasting and powerful influences in the helping group derive from those not present.

Acting Alone versus Acting Singly

Implicit in membership is the fact that one never acts singly, although one may act alone. To act singly is similar to behaving individually. To act alone, however, recognizes the person is a social being, even when not in the presence of others. George Herbert Mead's insight into this fact was of major importance in the development of social psychology and symbolic interactionist theory (Strauss, 1956). Mead set in motion the expansion of existing knowledge of human behavior in significantly new ways:

> The self, as that which can be object to itself, is essentially a social structure, and it arises in social experience. After a self has arisen, it in a certain sense provides for itself its social experiences, and so we can conceive of an absolutely solitary self. But it is impossible to conceive of a self arising outside of social experience. When it has arisen we can think of a person in solitary confinement for the rest of his life, but who still has himself as a companion, and is able to think and to converse with himself as he had communicated with others. (p. 204)

The term for the phenomenon Mead describes is *human sociality.* It implies membership with others. This is seen in the fact that even when one person acts alone, he or she is influenced by others and, in turn, influences others. How the person acts alone is determined by what he or she has learned from others.

The Consequences of Client Choices

This phenomenon of acting and being acted upon, of influencing and being influenced, is not an abstract notion. The members of the unseen groups to which the client belongs must live with the client's changed behavior. The same is true of the client. When clients present themselves to the members of their unseen group, members react to them differently. Consequently, the client has to come to terms with the changed responses of these significant others. These changes in the reactions of others to the client are played back in the helping group. In turn, they influence what happens in the helping group for as long as the client remains a member of it.

A Note about Seen and Unseen Group Influences in Nonclinical Social Work

Finally, there is no reason to conclude that the absent group occurs with less regularity in nonclinical social work. The influences of unseen groups are visible in community social work in that they articulate issues of personal power. The unseen group is visible, for example, in the competition among volunteers who seek advancement and social prestige through community work. It is also apparent in cooperative work in large organizations. In brief, it can be inferred in all those areas of the lives of members that indirectly bring into play processes, including conflictual ones, that may date back as far as early childhood.

While community social work is examined in detail in Chapter 6, it is important at this point to recognize that personal needs are expressed by committee members in their committee work (Janis, 1972). This expression of personal needs also occurs in other kinds of groups at this level, including administrative groups and community planning groups. The social worker member of such groups needs to keep this fact in mind, for the absent members of unseen groups may influence and decisively affect the quality of the group's work and its outcomes at the community level.

THE REQUIREMENTS OF BEING A CLIENT

There is one overriding theme in becoming a client member of a social work helping group that needs articulation. It is that to become a client requires exceptional behavior. Most people do not ordinarily expect to become social work clients. They do so only in unusual circumstances. These circumstances do not consist of the presence of problems in a person's life per se. Rather, they turn on the inability of the person or persons to handle the problems encountered without assistance from a stranger, namely the social worker.

Clientship means, therefore, that one adds to as well as modifies one's range of memberships and membership behaviors.

Unlike most other roles, however, the client role is not without stigma. It is not a neutral role like the easily accepted role one assumes by visiting a physician in the role of patient. The modification of membership to include the social work client role is usually a well-kept secret that the person does not reveal to others unless they are well trusted.

As already noted, being a client requires exposure of self to a stranger. For many people this requirement carries with it implications of weakness. While asking for help from social workers is not always viewed as an indication of inadequacy, especially when the occasion is injury or illness, needing help is not what most people would wish for themselves or for their children. Simply put, asking for help is not included in the list of American ideals, even though it is tolerated and, under certain circumstances, an acceptable type of membership. However it may be viewed, asking for help is not without its costs in self-esteem and in the esteem of others who may learn about it. Social welfare services may be and often are thought of as social utilities, but their meaning is far from neutral. Nor is asking for help, in the social sense of personal need, behavior akin to calling the utility company when one's electrical supply is disrupted.

Becoming a Client Member

There are a variety of things a person must do, and sometimes endure, in order to become a client. Much of what is taught by social workers to clients is tested out in the helping group.

It is fairly easy to reduce the complexities of becoming a client to a few, especially technical components. Simply stated, the client-to-be either makes application for social work services or, depending on the situation, is offered such services without having asked for them. An example of the former is the person who applies to a family agency for help with a parent–child problem. Examples of the latter are clients in hospitals who are seen by a social worker either because the social worker assumed the initiative or because a referral for social work help was made by a nurse or a physician. In addition, some clients are required to see a social worker by court order and often become clients against their wishes.

With the exceptions of very small children and those unable to communicate verbally, once a person becomes a social work client member, the client is expected to tell his or her story. In a purely technical sense, the client is expected to tell his story directly, honestly, and in ways that enable the social worker to understand the manner of help the client needs. What is sought is a proper fit between what the client presents and how the social worker responds. When this is achieved successfully, the social worker and the client together consider more closely what it is the client needs and wants and what the social worker can offer. The elaboration of the client's story is of great importance, because as the original version of the client's story expands its real meaning to both client and social worker begins to emerge. When this occurs, the membership of the client and social worker as a helping group takes on meaning.

The older image of the detached social worker who listens, makes a diagnosis, arrives at an intervention plan, and after that intervenes is largely one of historical interest, although vestiges of this approach survive. Today, however, the social worker does not wait with his or her interventions until the client's story is fully told. Intervention begins at the very outset of the work, when the social worker is an active participant in helping the client to elicit the story.

THE SKILLS OF CLIENTSHIP

A social role is a way of acting in given situations. It carries implications for others in similar or different roles. Each social role consists of certain expectations and behaviors. All occupants of given social roles are simultaneously holders of other social roles. For example, a man may be a worker in one place, a father in a second, a worshiper in a third, and a client in a fourth. In this instance, the roles the person occupies are worker, father (parent), worshiper, client.

The client role is most typically found in social agencies, although it is also found in hospitals, clinics, prisons, and increasingly in private practice offices of social workers. The professional social worker teaches the client how to be a client through his or her own behavior, for example, questions asked, responses given, praise and approval when the client demonstrates expected behaviors, and nonacceptance when the client demonstrates inappropriate behavior. Thus the social worker, overtly or subtly, teaches clients what is expected of them in the client role and acts approvingly when clients acquire and demonstrate competence in its discharge.

In this connection, the social worker transmits to clients the following behavioral prescriptions as they assume their roles in the problem-solving activities of the helping group: (1) the management of information; (2) the management of loss and social image; (3) the management of feelings; (4) the management of choice; (5) the management of consequences; and (6) the ability to transfer learning.

The Management of Information

The skills of information management run parallel to social interaction but are not the same. For example, the ability to hear what is said does not preclude lack of understanding or selective hearing, or even misinterpretation. Objective and subjective information processing are not quite the same thing. Many people do not consciously attend to such similarities and differences until it becomes important to do so. When a social worker says, "Perhaps you can recall what he said to you, and what you made of that," it may be the first time that a client becomes aware of the differences. However, allowing for wide variations, it is generally assumed that people do understand common definitions of situations. To conduct daily life with a minimum of rationality, for example, they must understand and agree on the meanings of words and other culturally significant symbols.

The ability to apply the skills of information management to the social work helping situation implies that client and social worker understand each other's language and that each is able to tell the other what he or she means and is talking about. Simultaneously, it is far too easy to assume that clients understand social workers, considering the wide variations among clients and social workers, such as social class, upbringing, majority and minority status, racial and ethnic variation, and educational background. The tasks that face innumerable clients in needing to learn the habits and language of their social workers in order to manage information generated in social worker–client interaction are complex and often difficult to master. Thus, the troubled client has the additional problem of learning to be a client through information management.

The Management of Loss and Social Image

Loss is a common experience, particularly evident among persons who seek help with personal problems. Yet the management of loss is not merely a matter of suffering, but of activity. Thus it can be thought of as a skill that is taught and learned. Most of this is accomplished in some form during childhood, and its meanings are transmitted by parents and other adults. Yet the universality of loss as a social phenomenon is only recognized when the loss suffered is significant, one involving a relative or close friend, for example. Among children, it is observable when a favorite animal dies.

With each loss there occurs not only mourning for what has been lost, be it a job, a relationship, or a person, but also the image of what one once was and might have been. The "might have been" has to do with mourning a future that was never quite realized because of the particular loss or losses involved. What was in the past is now the memory of previous times, which are characteristically recalled as happier times. It would be quite unusual if other persons, in addition to the client member, were not also involved in the mourning, for nothing happens in the lives of persons without social concomitants.

The link between membership and mourning rests on symbolization and internalization. The skill the client needs is to be able to face the meaning of the lost thing or person, both directly and indirectly. Where the loss is direct, as in the case of death, the client member needs to know how to grieve for that specific person; and the social worker must be able to help him or her do so when needed. Where there occurs the loss of a limb, the direct aspects of grief have to do with changed self-image concerning the body, and the indirect aspect has to be dealt with in terms of the meaning of the loss for the person's changed relationships with other members.

One way of dealing with loss is denial. Denial is a mechanism of defense of the ego, and it is one of the most common forms of managing unwelcome news or truths. Nor is denial necessarily undesirable; there are many good reasons why it might be better "not to know." Being faced directly with the probability of one's imminent death due to irreversible illness is a case in point for some people. At the same time, for some clients denial may hinder necessary planning for the future and for a good life beyond the loss sustained. For most people, mourning is a natural process and proceeds well without professional intervention. For the social work client the picture may look rather different. Here the problem is that the client is coming for help, presumably to make changes in his or her life. When these are hindered by the inability of clients to mourn their losses, this may in itself be the underlying reason for needing and seeking help. One example occurs among divorced persons who contemplate remarriage. Unless the former marriage and its failure are dealt with more or less verbally, the new relationship may suffer—the very reason the client seeks help. Often the remaining feelings are such that the verbalized issue has less to do with the new commitment than with the resolution of the old one. The point is that the losses of past accomplishment, of past relationship, and especially of the image of what the partners once hoped for must be faced, and the issues these losses pose must be resolved.

Nowhere is there a more telling illustration of the meaning of the membership "we" than in the dynamics of mourning. The aspect of social image change in loss and mourning can be a dramatic documentation of the changed circumstances it describes. Consider, for example, the woman who has lost her partner through death or divorce and who reports feeling left out of the social life she and her partner once enjoyed. She says that she was acceptable only to the extent that she was one of a pair. Similarly, widowers and divorced men are subject to attempts by others to change their current life state as single people. They receive offers to "match" them with others who might become new marriage partners.

The point is that loss, whether induced or spontaneous and unwanted, not only creates a different social image of the person or persons involved, but is also influenced, if not manipulated, by others. It is hoped that a new social image becomes available that is not only satisfactory to the person directly involved but also to others to whom he or she is significant. And unless the client member is to be something other than a mere recipient of impressions of others, the ability that the person needs is the ability to mourn and to become active in making only those choices about the present and the future that are based on careful consideration of one's options. The management of loss is a set of skills increasingly necessary for the millions of older people who, because of increasing longevity, will spend the remaining years of their lives without a partner.

Another kind of mourning has to do with the loss of health, or with an injury leading to permanent disability and its consequences. Consider the following case from hospital social work practice:

> As I came to visit Mr. Smith, the nurse was just leaving. In her hands she carried bandages she had changed on his leg. I had seen the client once before. He was a 37-year-old truck driver who had been in an accident and lost his right foot as a result. Mr. Smith recognized me immediately, calling me by my name. "Some mess," he said, and I agreed with him. He added "When it rains, it pours." I said, "So it's not only the foot, there are other troubles, too." Mr. Smith said that I must have been listening in when he and his wife were talking last night when she came to visit. Mr. Smith thinks that he has already lost his job. The company sent him 2 weeks' pay, and he has heard nothing since then. In rather rapid order, he talked about: Mrs. Smith wanting to go to work, which he does not like because, as he put it, a woman belongs at home; the house they were planning to buy; and their two teen-age boys. He worries about a court proceeding, but doesn't know when that would be, or whether there might be one at all. He worries about getting a job, and then said that maybe his company would give him an office job, but he doesn't really think they will.

There is a rambling and mildly disoriented quality about Mr. Smith. This is often a normal reaction to a major loss. He is worried, confused, uncertain—all understandable, realistic reactions in a fairly early stage of mourning for his losses. For the social worker there ought to arise the question of how soon these realistic concerns are to be addressed, particularly Mr. Smith's understandable eagerness to get back to work. The concrete needs, such as money, food, housing, and income, need immediate attention. Yet there must also be time for drawing on Mr. Smith's skills in grieving, to let him know that tears are acceptable, and to discuss with him whether and to what extent he thinks they are. Lack of attention to loss and its implications is a disservice to the thousands of clients who consider the display of grief to others and to themselves to be signs of weakness. Much disappointment in futile attempts at rehabilitation could be avoided were the necessary grief work that should precede or accompany it attended to more regularly than it seems to be. False reassurance that "everything will be all right" is a common mistake, whether it comes from the client and remains unchallenged, or whether the words are spoken by the social worker, the nurse, or the physician.

In addition to this complicated picture, the family's participation needs to be considered. Most social workers would bring Mrs. Smith into the work and, in this case, also the children, because they are components of the client's primary group and are clearly affected by Mr. Smith's injury. Their unspoken questions may include: "Why did you do it? Was it really your fault? Couldn't you have done something to avoid the accident?" Another frequent thought, equally unexpressed in words, is: "Look at what you did to me, to us, to the children." Here is the anger so often associated with loss and grief. For clients who feel too guilty to express such thoughts to the injured member, it is nevertheless necessary that they learn to come to terms with them and to express them without damage. The fact is, however, that often such considerations become lost in light of the immediacies of dealing with hospital bills, insurance reimbursements, and the tendency to substitute fast recovery measures for careful work by the clients (with help) around the long-term consequences of loss. The differences between a sense of well-being and being physically compromised are significant and must be dealt with skillfully.

The Management of Feelings

The management of feelings is usually linked to the ability to express the meaning of events. Words without feelings have limited persuasiveness or influence. In the absence of affective expression, the question always is: Did he or she really mean it? To have meaning, words of praise, anger, or other feelings must be accompanied by expressions of genuineness. Words alone are inadequate. While the client's ability to manage feelings is the expected behavior or the desired goal, many clients find this problematic, not only in the helping group but, even more significantly, in their relations to others elsewhere. Some clients may need permission to express feelings, particularly those feelings involving anger, love, sexual need, and desire.

On the other hand, there is little to be gained by the expression of feelings for their own sake. The expression should be tied to the reasons that underlie the client's request for help. There is a fine balance between teaching a client to express feelings that may be unacceptable to him or her and imposing the social worker's own views of cultural traditions and values that are by no means the same for all. There is a difference between learning the skill of saying what one means and learning to say things in ways that have little to offer when viewed in light of one's cultural, geographic, or ethnic identifications.

The skill of managing one's feelings is not confined to conversations with social workers or others. It has an aspect that is personal, that is to say internal, in the sense that persons talk to themselves. Guilt, anxiety, and fear are some of the inhabitants of the internal life, as are hope, anticipation, and optimism. At least some of the time, the client should be able to transcend the internal barriers that tell the client that feelings are better left unexpressed. Long experience in managing feelings in particular ways is not easily changed. Indeed, many a social worker has struggled with the question of helping the client manage his or her feelings without at the same time destroying something that is deep, important, and legitimate, that belongs to the client, including the client's right to manage as he or she sees fit.

The Management of Choice

In social work practice, a substantial amount of attention is given to decision making, the ability to make choices with respect to solutions to a wide range of human problems. The concern is not exclusively with the contents of particular choices, but with the skills that are needed, or need to be learned, to take the risks that are inevitably aspects of decision making. Common among many clients is an ambivalence based on a fear of making commitments. It is worth noting in this respect that some choices have greater consequences than others. That is, some choices are more characteristic of long-range commitments than others, while other choices are short-term in nature and easily reversed if necessary. Examples of the first category are choosing to have a life-endangering operation, choosing a marriage partner, and deciding on a professional career rather than on a job. Examples of less consequential choices include deciding where to spend one's vacation, what house to live in, and whether to accept employment in one firm or in another. Skill in making choices facilitates the use of professional help. It can also be learned in the process of using that help.

An important aspect of making choices has to do with the fact that decision making is always a social rather than an individual act. This is because the member is a social being and his or her actions have consequences, therefore, for others.

The Management of Consequences

The aspect of social work practice that illustrates the membership perspective more definitively than any other is the client's skill in managing the consequences of choices made with the aid of the social worker. It is in this connection that the differences between individualism and membership are clearest.

Essentially, dealing with the consequences of choices has to do with responsibility. In the framework of individualism, responsibility rests with the individual because it is thought that independence lies at the heart of the human condition. Everyday expressions, such as "each person hoes his own row," "you made your bed, now you must lie in it," and "it's your funeral" reflect the ethos of individualism. Independence becomes confused with autonomy, the latter being the ability to act with a sense of responsibility, with clear awareness of consequences.

While autonomy is a step further toward membership than individualism, it still implies that the consequences are individual in nature. The membership perspective holds that the consequences of deciding, of selecting among options, are personal, not individual; and that personalism is definable as an aspect of one's social nature. Thus, the skill of managing consequences rests on selecting from among a variety of possible alternatives. It requires that the person know how to evaluate evidence that points to preferences and how to weigh the possible outcomes in terms of their relative desirability.

The management of consequences is as much an attitudinal problem as it is an intellectual one. It is also linked to the perception of one's worth. There are many clients who think that they have no right to make their own decisions or, for that matter, no right to express preferences concerning their wishes. In essence, the question is this: "Given the way I act, how do I appear to you, and what do you think about me?" This is Cooley's (1912) well-known looking-glass concept. In the membership perspective, the looking-glass concept is of particular importance because it tells the client how his or her membership is perceived by fellow members and vice versa.

Choices, in the service of social self-determination, take into account both the person who chooses and others; both what is contributed by one's self and that which is contributed by others. This definition of choice may suggest a social constriction of behavior. Yet it can also be viewed as leading to freedom where, imbedded in a social milieu, persons can find reassurance and security, yet not without danger or fear.

Siporin (1982) argues that social work needs to reexamine its moral philosophy:

> In response to major social changes, the social work profession's moral philosophy and mission have become fragmented and weakened. Some social workers are being charged as "immoral." Official positions taken by professional organizations on certain moral issues are controversial and express a libertarian morality that is open to question and criticism. (p. 516)

Siporin's major point is that the profession cannot continue to work along lines of sole concern with what the client wants or should do for his or her sake alone, as if he or she lived in a social and moral vacuum. Membership holds that this concern is misplaced to begin with because all behavior is social. Furthermore, when social workers suggest that a client can live solely in accordance with his or her own needs or desires and without reference to his or her sociality, they unwittingly cause damage to their own profession, or at least distort it.

The Ability to Transfer Learning

It is reasonable to think of social work help as learning. The learning is not cognitive, as it is in school, but rather informal, as in a session with several client members at a time. This idea guided much of the early group work movement in social work, organized as it was around recreation and informal education.

Learning can also be readily detected in the work of one social worker and one client as partners. However one conceptualizes learning in social work, the assumption is nearly always that the social work helping group is a means, not an end in itself. The hope is that what the client member has learned in the helping group is transferable to other group situations. Most social workers would undoubtedly judge the effects of their efforts with clients by what happens, or does not happen, concurrent with and subsequent to the helping experience. It is for this reason that the abilities of clients are referred to as skill in the transfer of learning.

CONCLUSION

Clientship is conceived of as self-help for issues and problems of living for which the aid of the social worker is either desired or needed. To be realized, clientship depends on relationships with the social worker and, at times, with other clients. Its effects are always those that include, but are not confined to, the self. Clientship is, therefore, a membership role.

There are functions in the behavior of clients inherent in their role as self-helper that have to do with reporting, reenacting, and planning. These, in turn, may be linked to specific actions in becoming a client and to the skills of clientship, such as the management of information, the management of loss, the management of feelings, the management of choosing among options in order to make intelligent decisions, the management of the consequences of such choices, and, finally, the ability to transfer what has been learned in the social work helping group to the other aspects of daily living. It seems natural, then, that the next step in the development of the membership perspective of social work practice should be to consider the social worker as member.

In being subjected to the same universal rules of membership—constant connectedness and conditional accessibility—the social worker role is finally placed where it has not always been portrayed to be, namely inside the helping group. Varieties of formulations having to do with distance, professionalism, objectivity, and neutrality regarding the clinical social worker role in particular have left the matter somewhat in suspension. The membership perspective solves the problem, as the reader will see in the next chapter.

REFERENCES

Biestek, Felix P. (1957). *The casework relationship*. Chicago: Loyola University Press.

Carlton, T.O. (1984). *Clinical social work in health settings: A guide to professional practice with exemplars*. New York: Springer Publishing Company.

Cooley, J.H. (1912). *Human nature and the social order*. New York: Scribners.

Falck, H.S. (1981). *The "seen" and the "unseen" group in clinical social work*. Monograph #3 in the Health Social Work Practice Series. Richmond, VA: Virginia Organization of Health Care Social Workers.

Janis, I.L. (1972). *Victims of groupthink*. Boston: Houghton Mifflin.

Perlman, H.H. (1957). *Social casework: A problem-solving process*. Chicago: University of Chicago Press.

Perlman, H.H. (1979). *Relationship: The art of helping people*. Chicago: University of Chicago Press.

Robinson, V.P. (1930). *A changing psychology for social case work*. Chapel Hill: University of North Carolina Press.

Siporin, M. (1982). Moral philosophy in social work today. *Social Service Review, 56* (4), 516–538.

Strauss, A. (Ed.). (1956). *The social psychology of George Herbert Mead*. Chicago: University of Chicago Press.

Tropp, E. (1974). Three problematic concepts: *Client, help, worker. Social Casework, 55* (1), 19–29.

5 The Social Worker as Member

When Tropp (1974) examined the "three problematic concepts: *client, help, worker,*" he asserted that

> The concept of member is borrowed from group work, and it could very well become the most valued gift of group work to the entire profession. . . . A member knows he has rights; he does not wait upon someone's benevolence. (p. 28)

While Tropp's prediction has yet to be realized, it does underscore the need to attend to the role of the social worker as member, which is the purpose of this chapter. The question is, what kind of member is the social worker, and what are the attributes of that membership?

Tropp discussed the term "worker" (or social worker) because he thought it to be a "problematic one." In perhaps less urgent terms, so have most other social work theorists. In general, discussions of the worker have been undertaken within the client–social worker relationship. The examples provided in most textbooks, however, emphasize the interventions of the social worker.

In Chapter 4, the client role was systematically defined and described. The same approach is used in this chapter to define and describe the social worker as member. The assumption is that neither the client nor the social worker can be understood without reference to the other.

THE COMPONENTS OF SOCIAL WORK ACTIVITY

Five components define social work activity: (1) task relatedness, (2) use of knowledge, (3) rationality, (4) the conscious use of self, and (5) methodology. While it is possible to define the social worker's role in these terms irrespective of theoretical approach, it will be noted that the membership perspective is built into the consideration of each component in the sections that follow.

TASK RELATEDNESS

The fact that clients apply for, or are offered aid in the management of, membership implies the purposefulness of all social work activity. The task at hand must at all times be related to (1) the problem or situation for which the client seeks or is offered help, and (2) social work purpose. The fact that social work intervention has to do with everyday client experiences is much older than the preoccupation with intrapsychic phenomena currently found in clinical social work. In motivation, aid giving has ranged all the way from religious ideals to the largely secular humanism of the present day. Always, however, there is some sense of purpose at work, articulated regularly and at times dramatically in the development of the profession, both in England and the United States (Briggs & Macartney, 1984; Pacey, 1950; Pimlott, 1935; Tropp, 1977). The central idea has always been that clients visit social agencies for a reason, that there must be a visible relationship between the request for or offer of help and its outcomes. Thus, the social agency has always been regarded as a community service, a resource a community renders its members.

One might wish that asking for and accepting help from a community resource were as natural as the performance of other basic life functions, such as eating and sleeping. The seeking of aid, however, has always been associated with the unusual, a condition or situation in which the person cannot meet his or her own needs. The meeting of one's own needs has always been the preferred mode, and only in its absence has the acceptance of aid from others been justifiable.

From the very outset, from the preprofessional days of social work up to modern times, a dominant theme of the task-related character of the social services has been the struggle to meet unmet and often unmeetable needs with inadequate means. This was and is hardly a matter of accident. Indeed, many social workers think of the relations between clients and other members of the community as discriminatory, unjust, and punitive. This perception is reinforced by several factors: the shortage of adequately trained professional personnel; the lack of reasonable financial support for the social services; the inadequate and sometimes absent coordination of community services; and the inadequacy of facilities, especially institutional ones.

All of these problems also reflect a lack of social planning, despite major advances in social work research in recent years. This condition is most significant in its effects on all of social work. The profession still lacks important data, especially in regard to knowledge about the conditions of chronic dependency and the best solutions to it. Thus, social workers are usually forced to make the most of too little. As a result, the move toward greater clarity about what social workers can realistically do and not do is often reduced to an essentially defensive series of maneuvers. It involves working under conditions of compromise that leave little room for experimentation or the taking of prudent chances with new methods of intervention.

While there is no question that the size, scope, and influence of social work has grown as its knowledge, research, and methods have improved, there still exists a fine balance between the essentially positive achievements of the profession's major tasks and the negative societal factors that have caused it significant problems. This fact, as much as anything, documents the membership aspects of the profession, since whatever American society does or does not do for social work, it does for or to itself. To a degree, the ambivalence social workers themselves have expressed about their profession's shortcomings has been addressed by an increasing sense of accountability for their practice. Yet it is unrealistic to expect that better evaluation studies will allay their sense of ambivalence because such studies cannot resolve structural and ideological problems in American society with regard to seeking and accepting aid in the management of membership.

Another reason for the narrow definition of social work tasks is implicit in the belief that monies paid by taxpayers and volunteers to support social welfare are "gifts" to those who receive them and should therefore be used sparingly. One is entitled to be generous only with money individually earned and owned. A further implication is that the clients who use social services are using resources provided by other people who make social services possible. Thus clients are told, in effect, that the social agency, the social worker's skills, and the social worker's time are the property of everyone except the client. As a consequence each social worker must husband resources with care in order that (1) he or she may cover as many clients as possible, and (2) what others have provided through their labor is not misused. Thus, an overdetermined task orientation among social workers may unintentionally further the view that short-term services, highly structured and focused on immediate needs, are preferable to long-term work, not because one is inherently better than the other but because one is cheaper.

The step from belief in one's moral superiority as giver, rather than as recipient, to thoughts about the moral unworthiness of the social welfare client is a short one that is designed to distance the giver from the recipient. In comparison to the client who only uses but does not produce income, the central questions are these: "What do I get out of it?" and "What does the client take from me?" The underlying definition of the task is, therefore, to do what must be done but no more, and thus relieve the producer of services of the demands of the consumer. In contrast, the question the membership perspective poses is this: "What are the costs and gains that *we* incur in giving and in receiving?"

It is evident that the social worker, under whatever definition of membership, whether it accords with our ideals or not, functions in behalf of the best and the worst that defines the community. The social worker is its product and its agent. Educated, financed, and sanctioned by the community, the social worker represents in professional and personal terms the rather narrow and restrictive standards and values of American culture, even given its many internal variations. Whatever changes social workers might propose, alone or through their professional organizations, whether in the form of legislation or the modifications of social agency procedures, are nearly always made without questioning the system. Social work and social workers are in the main loyal to America's dominant, everyday values.

In sum, task relatedness rests on this tripartite set of realities that structure social work practice: that clients and social worker meet for specified purposes; that resources are kept inadequate compared to the complexity of the tasks to be performed; and that the moral judgments that attend giving and receiving help are such that elective charity (even in the case of taxes) rather than social obligation is the dominant motivation. Finally, American social workers lend credence to these rather restrictive attitudes toward task relatedness and morality, since they, too, are the products of the society that engenders and supports their work and their attitudes.

The questions about the role of the profession and about the social workers who are its members will find more effective resolution when American citizens, taxpayers, and the purveyors of a variety of value systems develop far more clearly than they have about what they are prepared to support in the field of social welfare. To date there is little evidence that such clarity is on the horizon, be it related to public education, medical and health care, the incarceration of ever-increasing numbers of people for crimes committed, and those others whom social workers as professionals and also as members of the community face on a daily basis.

THE USE OF KNOWLEDGE

All professions, including social work, rely heavily on the use of knowledge in order to perform their chosen functions. There are three essential areas of knowledge that influence social work practice. The first is knowledge about the behavior of clients in the context of membership. The second is knowledge about the allocation and division of human resources. The third is knowledge about the social worker as the professional member of the helping group. Besides these three areas of knowledge there are also large amounts of other data available to the social worker. They range from life cycle studies (Erikson, 1959), to studies about behavior in small groups (Feld &

Radin, 1982; Hare, 1976; Stogdill, 1974), to psychoanalytic, socio-logical, and philosophical investigations (Elson, 1986; Parsons, 1964; Rychlak, 1981; Smelser & Smelser, 1970; Specht & Craig, 1982). All have the potential of contributing to social work; yet only some can be utilized as presented in their original form. Social workers must first translate such knowledge into social work terms before it can be applied in work with clients.

The rationale for drawing on the vast knowledge about human beings is to find answers that are useful in helping clients. In the absence of studies that clearly demonstrate the efficacy of certain theoretical frameworks over those of others, practitioners are forced to rely on what works for them or on what fits their preferences on other than scientific grounds. This is not nearly as negative as it may at first sound, for the array of knowledge from which social workers can draw is rich and offers the opportunity for creativity. Because the social worker's effectiveness depends only in part on scientific knowledge, one must not overestimate the importance of comparisons. Yet, as Maluccio (1979) implies, some theory of human behavior is needed to organize one's work with a degree of consistency.

Knowledge of Client Behavior

It should be understood that this first category of knowledge includes vast amounts of data, ranging from the biological to the psychological, the social, and the philosophical. It is in this cate-gory that one finds the widest range of choices made by practitioners insofar as the use of that knowledge is concerned. It is also the most critical since the data or theories social workers choose influence the manner in which they assess the clients' situations and deter-mine the nature of intervention.

Given the diversity of data and theories available about nearly every aspect of human life, it becomes all the more important to find common denominators that organize what is known. In the membership perspective these denominators are the two principles of constant connectedness and of conditional accessibility. All of the diverse knowledge available is subsumable under these two membership principles discussed in Chapter 2. Thus, it is possible to consider numerous examples in each category of knowledge while maintaining the central focus of membership. Similarly, the two membership principles demonstrate how knowledge areas link to each other, making the boundaries among many fields of knowledge quite tentative. For example, it is impossible to consider personality, a psychological phenomenon, for very long without also considering social learning because personality is heavily influenced by what others, usually adults, have taught through their behaviors. To cite another example, it has long been known that certain inherited biological traits are associated with the development of certain mental illnesses, such as manic–depressive disorder. The manifestation of this psychiatric illness is behavioral: One can listen to the client, observe his or her behaviors, and make inferences in the form of assessment or diagnosis. Much the same can be said about the schizophrenias (Johnson, 1984). The main point, however, is that fewer and fewer behavioral conditions, be they pathological or not, can be explained by single theories that belong to a single field of knowledge.

The same kind of overlapping takes place in totally nonclinical, nonpathological aspects of life. For example, in international politics the powerful yet frequently overlooked personal needs of national leaders influence decisions that can potentially affect every human being on earth. In social work, the division between individual services and the environment has so far made it impossible to use knowledge available about both with any real degree of effectiveness. Thus, clinicians often undervalue most of what goes on beyond the individual, and community social workers act as if anything psychological has little to do with their work.

Stein (1963) addressed the relationship between knowledge from social science and other sources and asserted that ". . . social work is not applied social science; it is not even applied social, psychological, and biological science. Social work derives its knowledge from science but its spirit from philosophy, religion, ethics, moral values; and its method is derived, at least in part, from unexplored— and unexplorable—subtleties of human relationships. There is art in social work method precisely because it is not all science, and while we must strive constantly to enhance the scientific base of our work, we would not wish to, even if we could, eliminate the aesthetic or the ethical components" (p. 229).

The strain in professional social work is toward learning, toward intellectual self-consciousness, and toward the use of data whenever and wherever they are available. The former is necessary in order to make room for the latter. The accent on the former makes the activity of the social worker the performance of the expert. That is, despite all of the risks and uncertainties that are inherent in being a professional member of a social work helping group, one opts for a science base. Yet, the findings of Rogers (1962), of Truax and Carkhuff (1967), and of Maluccio (1979) suggest that there is no real conflict between the scientist-practitioner and the humanist-practitioner. They can be one and the same person (Lapham & Shevlin, 1986). Discriminative perceptiveness, emotional balance, generosity, scientific skepticism, and openness and candor in work with clients all fit together.

With these thoughts in mind, attention now shifts to another, closely related aspect of the knowledge social workers need in practice. This is knowledge about the allocation and division of human resources.

Knowledge of Human Resources

A second large area of knowledge of importance for the practice of social work is generally regarded as distinct from knowledge of human behavior. This knowledge is usually denoted by the heading of social policy. Included under this heading are social legislation, political process, and administrative rule making. From the membership perspective, however, this complex of principles, data, and research findings belongs under the heading of human behavior for the following reasons.

First, when viewed descriptively, knowledge of social policy tells us how and toward what ends members of a given society create and divide their common resources. Second, social welfare policy narrows the field to those concerns most important to social workers, namely how, in society, members treat other members who find themselves in need of help. Third, clarity about what is can lead to clarity about what ought to be. This is the moral aspect of resource division, and it reflects prevailing values. Fourth, the systematic study of how common resources are allocated is the first step in bringing about changes that benefit those to whom social workers are primarily committed, namely their clients.

As the matter stands, there is no discernible movement to unify the study of social policy and other areas of human behavior. The failure to do so may be traced to the same basic problem with which this book began, namely the profession's preoccupation with the individual. Consequently, the sociopolitical aspects of human behavior that membership considers of equal significance for the study of the human condition are relegated to vague notions about "environment" and "ecology" and given ancillary billing.

The membership perspective allows for no split between what appears to be purely personal and what seems to be public. In membership thought, all that occurs is public and personal at the same time. That is why social policy concerns are membership concerns and must be treated as such. Treating them in this way one avoids the tendency to think of policy making and administrative law as matters beyond the reach of members. Instead, they are viewed as expressions of the very memberships they regulate and, in some ways, promote. The regulations embodied in the Social Security Act, for example, affect the entire citizenry of the United States. As is always the case, attempts to influence this legislation and its administrative regulations sooner or later involves people acting on behalf of others in face-to-face groups.

Social workers need, therefore, to use all of their skills in meeting the difficult demands that legislative and administrative negotiation requires. They need to know not only what goes on in clinic and legislature, but also how to influence procedures and processes as an aspect of their daily work as social workers.

Knowledge of Social Worker Behavior

Knowledge about social worker behavior with clients is of central importance for the steady improvement of social work practice. One aspect of this is what social workers know about clients, while the other addresses what clients know and think about the social worker.

Most knowledge of social worker behavior comes from two sources. One is informal and occurs when clients are asked to evaluate the social worker's performance as part of the termination phase of the common work. The other source is research, particularly evaluation research, carefully designed with attention to problems of validity and reliability of instrumentation.

Of equal importance, however, is the nomenclature upon which all evaluative efforts rest. The membership perspective rejects the view that social work theorizing rests on the individual in some relation to the environment on scientific grounds. It follows that the evaluation researcher should assume, therefore, that what is being evaluated is the result of the interaction of two or more members, named client(s) and social worker. Indeed, Blythe and Briar (1987) recently wrote that more research is needed on work with families and other collections of individuals.

A further consideration in this regard has to do with how social workers describe their work with clients. Most social workers would agree that the work they do with clients is mutual in nature. At the same time, however, there is little visibility of this view when social workers are taught to "intervene in client systems." Even Maluccio (1979), whose tenor is humanistic, designates clients as "consumers" of services. One might observe that while one who intervenes with a consumer is nevertheless a member, it is a member whose self-description is more like that of an outsider than of a member of a helping group. Intervention speaks to what social workers do, while consumerism addresses the reactions of customers.

The term intervention implies the boundedness of individualism. Aside from the questionable application of military nomenclature to social work ("targets," "intervention," "systems"), there remains the need to understand what the members (clients and social workers) sought to achieve, how they went about it, and with what results. The joint work of two or more members places responsibility on each member, and by definition on all members. The fact that common efforts lead to common effects is consistent with the principles of constant connectedness and conditional accessibility. The evaluation of social work services, therefore, should address what clients and social workers achieve or fail to achieve together. It is the differences in their membership roles that justify the presence of both, and it is the membership behavior of the social worker, under carefully controlled conditions, that helps bring about whatever results are achieved. The responsibility rests on both members, even if it is unequal.

The major research issues the membership perspective must address are the definition of the variables in social work helping efforts and the evaluation of outcomes. While much information about clients is available, there is relatively little data available about the social worker member as practicing professional. Some data is available in episodic case reports and articles, and a list of social worker techniques derived from his research on group work has been developed by Shulman (1984). Blythe and Briar's (1987) discussion of "the major reviews of research on practice effectiveness in social work" (pp. 399–407) is also helpful in this regard. So is their conclusion that "although research on practice effectiveness has not yet generated a comprehensive array of interventive techniques, important strides have been made. Recent studies demonstrate the efficacy of social work" (p. 406).

One aspect of Maluccio's study (1979) on "interpersonal helping as viewed by clients and social workers" is of help to this discussion of the membership perspective in social work. The purpose of this qualitative study was "to contribute to the effectiveness of practice and service delivery by obtaining the clients' views on the interpersonal helping process and comparing these with the views of their social workers" (p. 23). Although Maluccio's sample consisted of only 33 clients and did not include the statistical analysis of data, certain significant or valid findings emerged.

Maluccio's findings support those of earlier studies in the field of counseling psychology (Carkhuff, 1969; Carkhuff & Truax, 1965; Rogers, 1962; Truax & Carkhuff, 1967). He found, for example, that the behavioral themes of "empathy or accurate understanding," "genuineness or authenticity," and "acceptance or nonpossessive warmth" are as applicable to effective social work practice as they are to other fields (p. 123). The importance of these behavioral variables has been widely cited in nonsocial work literature but has received only scant attention in social work (Fischer, 1973).

Maluccio, however, found four other behaviors that social workers need to communicate to clients if, in the views of clients, they are to be effective helpers. These are (1) "concreteness," which Maluccio defines as "the ability to communicate thoughts and ideas clearly and specifically"; (2) "competence," or the social worker's "proficiency in carrying out his or her professional role"; (3) "knowledge of human behavior"; and (4) "objectivity," or the "ability to see different points of view—being unbiased" (p. 123). Findings from the interviews Maluccio conducted with former clients consistently identified the desirability and helpfulness of these four dimensions of social worker behavior. Thus, it appears that the social worker's ability to project human attributes (empathy, genuineness, acceptance) are the most important variables leading to client satisfaction, providing they are communicated concretely, competently, knowledgeably, and objectively.

Maluccio's findings also suggest that social workers need to receive confirmation of their usefulness from their clients. In addition, social worker reluctance to ask for such confirmation, or to accept it when it is offered, highlights another aspect of social worker/client membership:

> [T]he findings suggest that there should also be examination of the impacts that clients have on workers. This is an area in which very little research has been conducted. Yet, in the study workers clearly came through as human beings who have personal needs and qualities and who are deeply affected by their clients and by what happens in their transactions with them. . . . There are indications that their clients' responses to them elicit positive or negative reactions that influence their sense of competence and role performance in a variety of ways. The workers' helping efforts are thus contingent upon the clients' personal impact on them. (pp. 189–190)

The further finding that "most clients are satisfied with the outcome," while social workers in most cases "are either dissatisfied or ambivalent" (p. 187), underlines the point just made. That is, in the common work of client and social worker, both need to give and both need to draw upon each other as participant members in a joint undertaking. The skills necessary to do so do not come easily, and they are not acquired automatically. As Maluccio observes, "The contract emerges as a much more complex concept than is reflected in the social work literature; it is not just an event or a product but also a dynamic process that influences the quality and outcome of the client–worker engagement in ways that need to be explored and understood further" (p. 187).

RATIONALITY

In turning to the role of reason in social work practice, it is necessary to repeat some of the ideas covered in the previous section on the use of knowledge in social work practice. However, instead of listing the knowledge sources social workers utilize, their logical qualities are explored here.

"Reason," writes A.R. Lacey (1976), "can be contrasted with revelation in religion, or with emotion and feelings as in ethics, but in philosophy it is usually contrasted with the senses (including introspection, but not intuitions)" (p. 181). Since social work in recent decades has evinced a great deal of interest in rationality as it affects the profession, the issue must be considered. This consideration is not simply a matter of whether social work is "scientific," for, as will be recalled, the membership perspective is based on phenomena such as biology and social interaction, which are observable, and on symbolization and the internalization of object relations, which rely on inference.

A major attribute of many professions is the aspiration to scientific status. The attainment of scientific credibility is seen as the means of entering that circle of professions that claim to be the "true" professions. Discussion about whether social work is a profession began with Flexner's (1915) somewhat self-contradictory address to the National Conference of Charities and Corrections in which he asserted with total assurance that social work was not a profession.

Flexner neither explained his qualifications to make such a judgment nor were they examined by social workers. They remained unchallenged for 68 years. It was not until 1983 that Austin pointed out that Flexner "began his address by questioning his competence to undertake the discussion because of his limited experience with social work literature and social workers" (p. 363). Thus, Austin was the first to note the contradiction between the claim to expertise inherent in Flexner's judgment and Flexner's self-confessed doubt that he was, in fact, qualified to render it. Austin also listed the key elements of a profession suggested by Flexner:

> Professions involve essentially intellectual operations with large individual responsibility, derive their raw material from science and learning, this material they work up to a practical and definite end,

possess an educationally communicable technique, tend to self-organization, and are becoming increasingly altruistic in motivation. (p. 363)

The emphasis on science and learning as a major basis for professionalism, balanced with self-responsibility and altruism, are also the hallmarks of rational thought and practice. Flexner asserted that social work had not achieved these characteristics and therefore, in his judgment, did not qualify for the status of "profession." Felix Frankfurter (1915), later Associate Justice of the Supreme Court of the United States, however, followed Flexner's address with one of his own, and concluded that social work, by following the traditions of the law, was a profession and should enter the universities.

The issue raised by Flexner's address of primary interest here is whether social work has or perhaps even should meet the standards of what he thought the hallmarks of professionalism to be. Should social workers, for example, be expected to "derive their raw material from science and learning"? The answer after 1915 was a reluctant "yes," and social work gradually ascended the high road to science-based professionalism.

This status was not achieved without cost, as social work's more recent weddedness to logical positivism in its research and education suggests (Brekke, 1986; Gyarfas, 1983; Heineman, 1981; Hudson, 1978, 1982; Schuerman, 1982).

Often overlooked in the history of social work, however, is the influence of science in the shift of the social worker from "do-gooder" to professional practitioner who values data, logic, careful inference, and proof, in short, intellectual accountability. Aided by such theorists as Perlman (1957), who demonstrated that problem solving in social work runs parallel to scientific method, the profession slowly began its move toward the rationality and logic associated with science, albeit not without resistance.

Although rarely documented, there has been an undercurrent of protest against a scientific base for social work, particularly by its clinical practitioners. Their criticism has had to do with the deemphasis in science-based practice models of the subjective elements of the social worker–client relationship and its hard-to-measure events or process. In addition, social work clinicians have been critical of the inability of social work scientists to evaluate social work as it is practiced, without the distortions that make it more amenable to investigation. Nevertheless, there can be no doubt that the research movement in social work has contributed to the increased effectiveness of social workers. Awareness that reason with its science-bound rules of evidence is applicable to social work practice has grown among social workers, as has acceptance of the fact that social workers are accountable to other members of the community who support their work through taxes or tax-deductible voluntary contributions.

Thus, social work has traveled a long way from the days of precept and example and the mystique with which the social work interview was associated for so many years. Franklin (1986) views Richmond as pivotal in the transformation of social work from "moral certainty" to "rational inquiry." In doing so, however, scientific social work, in its positivistic mode, replaced the earlier mystique by creating one of its own.

The lesson to be drawn from these considerations is that social work is sophisticated enough to select and formulate its own data base, to use knowledge from other fields appropriately, particularly the basic sciences, and to delineate what social work is and can be. Today's social workers think broadly; they do not merely add up various source materials. True progress is achieved when social work itself selects knowledge and synthesizes it to develop social work theory. The ultimate source of its theory is that vast knowledge about human behavior; the end result is the synthesized statement that leads to practice theory. This is the rational kernel in social work, the central core without which social work would not be a profession.

In sum, it is necessary that social work define its own practice. The step that leads to that definition is the identification of those human behavior variables from which social work practice principles are formulated. In the membership perspective these are as follows: that cells are semipermeable; that people select and monitor the way they interact with others; that people internalize their relationships with others; and that they assign meaning to their experiences. All these are known phenomena of human behavior, and from them many lower-order inferences can be drawn to further develop social work practice theory. The common denominators that underlie them are the dual principles of constant connectedness and conditional accessibility. Thus, it is not necessary to argue that one ought to believe in the membership perspective. Membership is fact. The membership perspective of social work rests, therefore, on an empirical base.

Implicit in the membership perspective, especially in relation to the social work role, is a commitment to rationality. This commitment subsumes positivistic, empirically based science, but it also includes the subjectivism of symbolic interactionism, as does any approach that rests on the careful and thoughtful collection and evaluation of interactional data. This is what effective social work requires. Thus, each professional social worker must be able to identify and select data and knowledge that are most relevant to the work being done and at the same time be aware of the scientific standing of that knowledge. An additional consideration has to do with the current indiscriminate use of technical language. Here, too, rationality needs to be the guiding concern, so that social workers identify and employ words and symbols that clearly define social work and are recognized for doing so.

Neither rationality as a human attribute nor rational professional behavior comes spontaneously. Rationality requires self-discipline.

THE CONSCIOUS USE OF SELF

The conscious use of self, as a concept, refers to those social worker behaviors that are the product of emotional and intellectual self-observation. This self-observation is purposeful. It is designed to produce self-control over one's actions as the social work member of the helping group. Its ultimate aim is to monitor one's usefulness to the client member.

In many important ways, the conscious use of self is a psychological phenomenon that addresses transference and countertransference issues that may either obstruct or facilitate the helping process (Hollis & Woods, 1981, p. 295). Of concern are those aspects of social worker behavior that fall into the realm of the unconscious, that realm where their effects upon rendering help are uncontrolled, yet potentially important. While the transference terminology is usually associated with clinical social work, coming as it does from psychoanalysis, failure to use it in other areas of practice is a serious omission.

Potentially all relationships, including all *professional* relationships, are subject to unconscious exploitation by a person for his or her own purposes. Becoming aware means taking control, making choices about what is said and done. Transference phenomena are overlooked when the subject matter and the task to be accomplished are stressed to such a degree that the process that can defeat them is ignored. Tragic mistakes have been made at the highest levels of government when decisions have rested on irrational factors, such as personal, psychologically determined needs that, in theory, have little to do with the subject matter being discussed (Janis, 1972). Community social work, because of its bias against anything "clinical," persistently ignores these factors. Transference phenomena express themselves in the attitudes social workers develop about all kinds of clients, in all varieties of settings, and which, when acted on, obstruct and hinder effective social worker performance. They are subject to recognition and awareness through supervision, consultation, and examined experience.

The conscious use of self, however, is not confined to countertransference issues alone. Another aspect of it is intellectual. The possession of knowledge is not, for example, the same as the appropriateness of the use one makes of it. And, since social work is a practical undertaking, the proper use of knowledge is one of the contributions the social worker member makes to the helping group. The point is that knowledge does not remain a neutral phenomenon with a life of its own. Rather, it is reflected in the emotional self-discipline and intellectual sophistication that the social worker displays to the client.

A third component of the conscious use of self involves the selection of techniques, that is, choosing the right interventions from a variety of options. Since this is discussed at length in the next chapter, the point to be made here is that the social worker possesses autonomy that is constantly demonstrated by asking, "What is the proper thing to do at this moment with this or with these clients?" Considerations that address the conscious delineation of intervention plans are as applicable to short-term interventions as they are to long-range ones. The point is that the emotional, intellectual, and technical aspects of social work are subject to the conscious, rational, and planful use of oneself as a social worker member, with and on behalf of the client member(s) of the helping group.

Despite the tendency to associate self-discipline with individualism, the picture of the self-disciplined member of the helping group does not call for withdrawal into a walled-off separatism from the clients. Rather, the membership of all who experience each other underlies the conscious use of self. Thus, the social worker's conscious use of self is necessary *because* he or she is a member. Were social workers individuals, there would be less need than there is to attend to the nature of both the conscious and the unconscious messages one sends clients. The conscious use of self is the social worker's effort to bring task-determined order into the qualities of professional memberships. Most, if not all, professional social work practice rests on this premise.

METHODOLOGY IN SOCIAL WORK PRACTICE

Social work has been both praised and taken to task for its concern with methods (casework, group work, community organization). Carroll (1977), for example, pointed out that " . . . no concept in social work practice. . . has generated more debate, has more often been declared useless, but has been more enduring than 'methods' formulation" (p. 429).

Social casework and social group work methodology addresses immediate interaction between and among clients and social workers. In community organization there are no face-to-face client–social worker interactions in the same sense as in the other two. In community organization the social worker works on behalf of large social groups such as a neighborhood, city, entire population. Yet there is a face-to-face group in community social work, a secondary group, in which members act on behalf of the unseen, tertiary groups just mentioned. Here too, just as in clinical social work, the social worker must be able to act significantly. This is the link to methodology, a set of techniques carefully selected as appropriate interventions for specific situations. In this connection, Carroll presents a three-part schema. The first part addresses the obvious need for nine "social technologies": (1) social planning; (2) community organization; (3) research; (4) supervision; (5) consultation; (6) administration; (7) group work; (8) family therapy; and (9) casework. Carroll's second category consists of seven "social units of concern": (1) individuals;

(2) families; (3) small groups; (4) formal organizations; (5) communities; (6) regions; and (7) societies. Her schema is completed with the category "social problems." These include poverty, drug abuse, and racial discrimination, to name only a few. While Carroll's schema is comprehensive, her "three-dimensional model of social work practice" falls short of informing the social worker about who it is, among "the social units of concern," that will be sitting or standing across from the social worker to receive social work help.

Methodology presupposes identifiable people. What is shared with and among them is membership behavior, and unless the dimensions of that behavior are clear, what the social worker member contributes is equally unclear. One cannot intervene in an abstraction. Thus, the social worker and the client are reviewed as persons who influence each other through their behaviors. The techniques selected by the social worker member are designed to bring about changes in the behaviors of clients who can be seen, named, and described in terms of what they do. At the level of technique, it is concreteness that is both needed and counts. Technique is the most empirically meaningful display of social work intervention. It is technique that gets things done.

If it is clear that social work practice is described by concrete, observable behavior and that the social worker is a member of the helping group, it is also clear that theory and other knowledge are the servants, not the masters, of the social work undertaking. This holds for theory in both the inductive and the deductive sense. In the former, repeated practice leads to generalizations and, in time, to testable hypotheses. In the latter sense, deduction relies on generalizations to be tested in practice over time. Here the social worker asks the questions about what has been learned from prior experience (his or her own or that of others) that may be applicable in the present case. This formulation may appear simple, but it is not. Indeed, it is the source of some of the most difficult intellectual problems the professional social worker faces. One reason for the difficulty is that the relationships between principles and practice are not linear, one-to-one matches. More goes into practice technique than silent, tacit reference to theory. Furthermore, the links between theory and practice are not always clear in every given situation. Oversimplified statements about induction and deduction merely whet the appetite for further investigation and simultaneously underline the need for more rational practice.

CONCLUSION

The components of social work as membership activity are task relatedness, the use of knowledge about social workers and clients, rationality, the conscious use of self, and methodology. What emerges from consideration of these components is the image of the social worker as a person who can relate to other people in a manner that promises to be disciplined, helpful, schooled in knowledge about human behavior, rational, informed by scientific skepticism, and clearly wedded to a technical repertory that can be taught, learned, and applied.

This chapter has shown as clearly as any other how a member can make qualitative choices regarding his or her membership. Under conditions of constant connectedness, the principle of conditional accessibility was operationalized by way of clarifying the actions and interventions of the social worker. As we shall return to this topic later in this book, no more needs to be said about it at this point.

REFERENCES

Austin, D.M. (1983). The Flexner myth and the history of social work. *Social Service Review, 57* (3), 357–377.

Blythe, B.J., & Briar, S. (1987). Direct practice effectiveness. In A. Minahan (Ed.-in-chief), *Encyclopedia of social work* (18th ed.) (Vol. I, pp. 399–407). Silver Spring, MD: National Association of Social Workers.

Brekke, J.S. (1986). Scientific imperatives in social work research: Pluralism is not skepticism. *Social Service Review, 60* (4), 538–554.

Briggs, A., & Macartney, A. (1984). *Toynbee hall: The first hundred years.* London: Routledge and Kegan Paul.

Carkhuff, R.R. (1969). *Helping and human relations* (Vols. I & II). New York: Holt, Rinehart and Winston.

Carkhuff, R.R., & Truax, C.B. (1965). Training in counseling and psychotherapy: An evaluation of an integrated didactic and experiential approach. *Journal of Counseling Psychology, 29* (4), 333–336.

Carroll, N.K. (1977). Three-dimensional model of social work practice. *Social Work, 22* (5), 428–432.

Elson, M. (1986). *Self psychology in clinical social work.* New York: W.W. Norton.

Erikson, E.H. (1959). Identity and the life cycle. *Psychological Issues, 1* (1), 50–100.

Feld, S., & Radin, N. (1982). *Social psychology for social work and the mental health professions.* New York: Columbia University Press.

Fischer, J. (1973). *Interpersonal helping: Emerging approaches for social work practice.* Springfield, IL: Charles C. Thomas.

Flexner, A. (1915). Is social work a profession? *Proceedings of the national conference of charities and corrections* (pp. 576–590). Chicago: Hildman Printing Company.

Frankfurter, F. (1915). Social work and professional training. *Proceedings of the national conference of charities and corrections* (pp. 591–596). Chicago: Hildman Printing Company.

Franklin, D.L. (1986). Mary Richmond and Jane Addams: From moral certainty to rational inquiry in social work practice. *Social Service Review, 60* (4), 504–525.

Gyarfas, M.G. (1983). Debate with authors: The scientific imperative again. *Social Service Review, 57* (1), 149–150.

Hare, A.P. (1976). *Handbook of small group research* (2nd ed.). New York: Free Press.

Heineman, M.B. (1981). The obsolete scientific imperative in social work research. *Social Service Review, 55* (3), 371–397.

Hollis, F., & Woods, M.E. (1981). *Casework: A psychosocial therapy* (3rd ed.). New York: Random House.

Hudson, W.W. (1978). First axioms of treatment. *Social Work, 23* (1), 65.

Hudson, W.W. (1982). Scientific imperative in social work research and practice. *Social Service Review, 56* (2), 256–258.

Janis, I.L. (1972). *Victims of groupthink.* Boston: Houghton Mifflin.

Johnson, H. (1984). The biological bases of psychopathology. In F.J. Turner (Ed.), *Adult psychopathology: A social work perspective.* New York: Free Press.

Lacey, A.R. (1976). *A dictionary of philosophy.* London: Routledge and Kegan Paul.

Lapham, E.V., & Shevlin, K.M. (Eds.). (1986). *The impact of chronic illness on psychosocial stages of human development.* Washington, DC:

Georgetown University Hospital and Medical Center, Department of Social Work.

Maluccio, A.N. (1979). *Learning from clients.* New York: Free Press.

Pacey, L.M. (1950). *Readings in the development of settlement work.* New York: Association Press.

Parsons, T. (1964). *Social structure and personality.* New York: Free Press.

Perlman, H.H. (1957). *Social casework: A problem-solving process.* Chicago: University of Chicago Press.

Pimlott, J.A.R. (1935). *Toynbee hall: Fifty years of social progress.* London: J.M. Dent & Sons.

Rogers, C. (1962). The interpersonal relationships: The core of guidance. *Harvard Educational Review, 32* (4), 416–429.

Rychlak, J.F. (1981). *A philosophy of science for personality theory.* Malabar, FL: Robert E. Krieger.

Schuerman, J.R. (1982). Debate with authors: The scientific imperative in social work research. *Social Service Review, 56* (1), 144–146.

Shulman, L. (1984). *The skills of helping individuals and groups* (2nd ed.) Itasca, IL: F.E. Peacock.

Smelser, N.J., & Smelser, W.T. (1970). *Personality and social systems* (2nd ed.). New York: Wiley.

Specht, R., & Craig, G.J. (1982). *Human development: A social work perspective.* Englewood Cliffs, NJ: Prentice-Hall.

Stein, H. (1963). The concept of the social environment in social work practice. In H.J. Parad & R. Miller (Eds.), *Ego-oriented casework: Problems and perspectives* (pp. 65–72). New York: Family Service Association of America.

Stogdill, R.M. (1974). *Handbook of leadership.* New York: Free Press.

Tropp, E. (1974). Three problematic concepts: *Client, help, worker. Social Casework, 55* (1), 19–29.

Tropp, E. (1977). *A humanistic foundation for social group work.* Richmond, VA: Virginia Commonwealth University School of Social Work.

Truax, C.B., & Carkhuff, R.R. (1967). *Towards effective counseling and psychotherapy.* Chicago: Aldine.

6 The Social Worker and the Client I

The roles of the social work member and the client member were discussed in the two previous chapters. Although these two roles are inseparable in practice, they are not identical. They were treated, therefore, as two distinct topics. However, in real exchanges between and among clients and social workers, such separations do not exist, not even for the sake of clarity and distinctiveness.

In this chapter and the next, the focus is on the functions that both members perform *together* even while their role differences are maintained. It is helpful in this regard to clarify a basic assumption that underlies this analysis. It is that each member addresses both the self and other(s). The social worker observes his or her behavior toward the client(s), and in principle, as in practice, the client does the same. Thus, there occurs a kind of self-monitoring as one speaks and acts, and a simultaneous monitoring of the other or others.

This multiple monitoring is a universal phenomenon that depends less on the particular role one plays than on the fact that others are meaningful. This does not mean one likes, approves of, or wants to behave as the other person. It does mean that the other is meaningful, that his or her behavior has symbolic value to all who are engaged in it or by it. Once again, this reflects the fundamental components of membership: constant connectedness and conditional accessibility. People who experience each other are members; membership is subject to selectivity, and its qualities can be influenced and changed.

In sum, the assumption is that both clients and social workers perceive each other as drawing inferences from what they communicate to each other. The client draws inferences about what the social worker is assumed to think; similarly, the social worker draws inferences regarding what the client might understand from the communication. As a result, each participant owns some of the behavior of the other, at least to the extent that each is capable of empathy, of sensing something about the condition of the other, and caring enough to do so (Keefe, 1976). For most people, this is a necessary condition for any kind of human relationship, from the superficial to the profound.

An immediately apparent implication of mutual interventions by social workers and clients is that clients intervene with themselves as they speak with their social worker(s) and that social workers do the same as they direct their attention to their clients. Each member helps his or her own role performance as each interacts with the other. The boundaries between and among them are permeable; there is access to the other and to the self simultaneously. This addressing of oneself as one speaks to the other is characterized by self-conscious monitoring, by awareness, and by impressions of how one "comes across."

This interactional process describes the simultaneous work of social worker and client. And it is indeed simultaneous, since listening and watching are activities that take place while the other(s) is engaged in concurrent, but also different, activity such as speaking, moving in the chair, smiling, crying, considering options. Both act, even though some activity may be sequential or in an alternating mode. In speaking, for example, one usually waits to speak until the other has finished. This does not mean that only the speaker acts at any given time. Both, or all, parties are active participants. Thus, all constantly intervene with each other (i.e., the social worker through social work intervention, the clients through client intervention).

THE CONTENT OF SOCIAL WORK INTERVENTION

The social work helping group is created to aid the client in the many possible tasks that are involved in managing his or her memberships. This means that (1) the tasks to be addressed are mutually definable by social worker and client(s); (2) the helping group itself consists of members; and (3) members are social rather than individual beings.

Clients have the potential for asking for and receiving many kinds of help from a variety of helpers. Why they ask for and receive social work aid depends not only on what they desire or need, but also on what the social worker can provide. Since social work offers help in the examination and meeting of *defined* needs, there must be a common, basic theme. The theme is that the problems the clients bring to social workers are social in nature; therefore, the interventions must be social and the outcomes must be measurable in social terms. In other words, social work addresses the management of membership, the social arrangement between and among people, as viewed in interactional terms. Hence, the assessment of social conditions must lead to interventions that modify these conditions toward ends desired by clients, while at the same time attending to the consequences of these changes as they affect and have meaning for others.

In this connection, it is interesting to note that social work's long history of formulating clients' problems, not in social but in individual terms, can be seen in the medicalization of problems, interventions, and the measurement of outcomes. When problems are formulated in social terms, however, quite different consequences become visible. The term "treatment," as compared to "aid in the management of membership," for example, points to the sharp contrast between essentially individualized, medical ways and social work ways of thinking and expression.

When one needs or thinks one needs medical treatment, one ordinarily visits a physician or someone who practices like a physician. Consequently, the problem one presents is an illness or an illness-like situation. As such it is viewed by patient and physician as an exceptional situation that, at a minimum, ought to be alleviated, and ideally cured. Unless it is chronic, illness is viewed as an event, rather than as a process. Attempts by physicians to shift the responsibility for illness to patients have generally failed because the condition at the level of presentation, be it for diagnosis, treatment, alleviation, or cure, calls for the knowledge and the skill of a professional medical practitioner.

In contrast, the assumption in the management of membership is that *social* problems often have no precise beginning, and even when they do, they rarely run the kind of time sequence or course implicit in disease. Social work does not address medical events; its main purpose is to help clients come to terms with everyday life situations. While it is true that one may not need a social worker's aid every day, it is nevertheless true that when one does, it is not so much the problem that is so unusual as it is one's inability to deal with it creatively. Dying is an everyday occurrence, even for those who face the death of a loved one for the first time. Raising one's children is common, yet one may need help to know what to do with one's anger about a child's behavior. Marital stress is practically universal, but learning to deal with it satisfactorily may require help. Social work is less a matter of addressing the unusual problem than the limited abilities of many people to manage satisfactorily what these common situations require. Rendering aid in the management of membership is, therefore, the central concern and activity of social work.

An extension of this argument has to do with the nature of suffering. Social work in the membership perspective assumes that suffering, too, is universal and, although highly undesirable in its immediate effects, cannot be altogether eliminated. While unnecessary suffering cannot be supported, it is in the nature of human life that suffering occurs to all in some way. Therefore, the management of that suffering needs to be taught and learned. The illusion of a social world without pain is just that, an illusion. In the membership perspective the position is taken that social work addresses the management of pain and suffering, rather than whether or not they exist. The focus is on the social concomitants of suffering, such as being poverty-stricken, being mistreated because of a criminal conviction, or being of the "wrong" religious persuasion, race, or ethnic group. The social management of suffering is an obvious need for those who are chronically ill or disabled. None of these problems falls in the realm of social work activity because there may be a physical or psychiatric illness involved; the reason these problems are amenable to social work intervention is that such conditions affect, sometimes in serious ways, the social memberships of people. Many of those involved are relatives, friends, and co-workers of the person; and they are also "afflicted" in some way, even if only secondarily.

Furthermore, the membership perspective does not tolerate unattended injustice, nor does it tolerate merely dealing with the effects of injustice. To manage one's memberships to the common benefit of oneself and others includes the removal of injustice. One way to learn to attend to pain is to lessen its source. When, therefore, social workers and clients ask what can be done, it is not only for abstract reasons. Rather, it is because one need not suffer silently and alone. The situation leading to the pain, suffering, or injustice can be changed.

The content of social work helping is subject to variation and exception. Indeed, there may be occasions when the problems clients bring to the social worker are self-contained in terms of time and circumstance. There may even be problems that do not really affect others, although it is difficult to identify such problems. The main point, however, is that there is little, if any, behavior that is not social or biosocial in origin. This is the main reason that the social work profession's focus of intervention is so wide-ranging and so often appears to be rather diffuse, especially to non-social workers. What binds social work's widespread activities together are identifiable common denominators of sufficient accuracy that they can be productively generalized to a range of concerns. The membership perspective offers such common denominators.

STYLES OF SOCIAL WORK INTERVENTION

Social work (and client) intervention can be viewed from a variety of standpoints. One has to do with technique, another with the cultural impacts on the process of giving and of taking aid, and the third with the dimensions used to assess client behavior. In this chapter we treat the first two, leaving the discussion of the third for the next chapter. None of the three styles should be considered in terms of priority in time or significance. All are significant and all are interlinked with each other.

TECHNIQUES

Monitoring

The most universal and commonly used social work technique is monitoring. The purpose of monitoring is to track, as much as possible, what is happening in the process of giving and taking aid. Although done in different ways and for somewhat different yet related purposes, both clients and social workers monitor.

From the standpoint of the professional, monitoring raises the social worker's awareness of the clients' habitual ways of dealing with issues as they arise in the work being done. They are "markers" in the client's behavior calling for social worker intervention. In fact, they also actualize the social worker's awareness of his or her own countertransference management, as discussed in Chapter 5.

Clients, too, monitor their behavior. They form opinions, reactions, and views about how they appear to the social worker, to other clients, and to themselves. When called upon, they are quite ready to say how the work is going. For example:

SOCIAL WORKER: Let's see where we are.
        CLIENT: We've been talking about my finding a job.

OR

SOCIAL WORKER: We also ought to talk about the amount of time we have left.
        CLIENT: One hour.

OR

        CLIENT: As I came here today, I suddenly realized that today is the last time our group will be together.
SOCIAL WORKER: We did a lot of work together.

In all three illustrations there is either awareness or evidence of monitoring of what is happening. Even when such awareness is not overt, the material can be readily brought to the level of awareness with a minimum of stimulation by the social worker. Members observe themselves and each other, and do so constantly.

Clarification

Carlton (1984) defines clarification as "a technique used to enhance the client member's ability to perceive himself in relation to others" (p. 118). The following example illustrates this technique.

The client, Mr. R., is an 80-year-old man, the father of two sons, whose wife is chronically ill. Mr. and Mrs. R. rely on the older of the two sons and his family for most of their needs. Their daughter-in-law does most of their shopping. Mr. R.'s conversation with the family agency social worker is a clarification of their situation as he perceives it.

> MR. R.: I told him that his parents are like most other older people, ignored by their own children. He yelled at me and said that his Mom and I are thankless and don't appreciate the fact that he and his family are constantly helping us.
>
> SOCIAL WORKER: And you said?
>
> MR. R.: I told him that he is a bald-faced liar and that I have not seen or heard from him in weeks.
>
> SOCIAL WORKER: What did he do?
>
> MR. R.: He insisted he was right and I was wrong and then he left by slamming the door and yelling that he didn't have to take treatment like that.
>
> SOCIAL WORKER: You told me a while back that you son calls or drops by nearly every day. But now you seem to think that he ignores and rejects you because you feel old.
>
> MR. R.: Oh, he comes over all right, but when he does, he tells us what to do all the time.
>
> SOCIAL WORKER: Maybe now we are talking about the real problem. Maybe it is not that your son ignores you. but that you feel mistreated.
>
> MR. R.: That is exactly the way it is.

Clarification, in this case, amounts to the mutual discovery by Mr. R. and the social worker of what really happens in the objective sense ("it is not that your son ignores you") and what Mr. R. experiences ("it is that you feel mistreated"). It should be noted that Mr. R. and the social worker are mutual participants in the clarification of Mr. R.'s situation. The clarification of the difference between being ignored and feeling mistreated is evident. It is also important in helping Mr. R. to face the true nature of his conflict with his son and what he can do about it.

Confrontation

According to Carlton (1984), confrontation "challenges the client behavior in a direct way. . . . [T]he general function of confrontation is to withdraw support for negative behavior" (p. 118).

What follows is an example of confrontation in which both the client and the social worker participate.

MR. R.: . . . and so he constantly tells us that we are old and lack the judgment we once had to make intelligent decisions. He constantly tells us that we are stupid, just because we are old.

SOCIAL WORKER: When you say "we" you mean your wife and you?

MR. R.: That's right. I got to take care of her because she is sick and can't speak for herself.

SOCIAL WORKER: I don't quite get what you mean.

MR. R.: When you get into your seventies—well, you know what happens [pointing to his head]—you get sort of weak up there.

SOCIAL WORKER: It sounds like you do the same thing to your wife that you complain about your son doing to you—only in a different way.

MR. R.: Whose side are you on? I thought you understood me.

SOCIAL WORKER: I think I do, and I think you do, too. And that's what hurts you.

Confrontation, in its proper use, rests on the material the client furnishes to the social worker and, when there is more than one client, to each other. Furnishing the data upon which the appropriate use of the technique must rest is, therefore, the client's contribution to the helping effort. The interpretation of the material, however, comes from the social worker.

The next example of the use of technique also illustrates confrontation, but in this example it is the client who confronts himself. He is able to do this on the basis of the previous work done with the social worker and what it has taught him about himself.

MR. R.: . . . and so I did it again, despite the promise I made to myself that I would not let him get me to yell at him [Mr. R. is speaking of his son].

SOCIAL WORKER: You must have forgotten for a moment.

MR. R.: No, I didn't. It was just that I was so mad that I wanted to hit him.

SOCIAL WORKER: You often describe yourself as a peaceful person; you once told me that good Christians don't go around hurting other people.

MR. R.: Don't you believe it; sometimes when I get steamed up, I could kill the. . .

Counseling

It is doubtful that Mr. R. could have spoken in this vein very much earlier. One may gain a sense of how true this is when the client and social worker counsel together regarding some of the arrangements that need to be made after Mr. and Mrs. R. have decided that they should "buy their way" (Mr. R?s words) into a home for the aged.

MR. R.: And so we decided that we have to face it.

SOCIAL WORKER: I feel uncomfortable about your wife not being here when you and I talk about her future and yours. I think we should get her in here before we go much further with your planning.

MR. R.: She knows all right, that I've been talking to you; she doesn't mind. But if you insist, I'll bring her.

SOCIAL WORKER: That's not quite the point. I think that if she feels that she does not have a part in the decision, she may—even if she agrees with you—also think that you did it to her.

MR. R.: Did what?

SOCIAL WORKER: Let's talk about what it means to give up home, I mean hers and yours.

Facilitation

Carlton defines facilitation, another common social work technique, in these words: Facilitation "is used to modify negative interactions in a positive direction and to affirm positive progress. Its use promotes and enhances membership connections and guides member interaction toward task accomplishment and goal attainment" (p. 121).

In the following illustration, Mr. and Mrs. R. and their social worker are discussing the practical problems of moving to the home for the aged. Their son Mr. R., Jr. is present.

MR. R.: Junior and his mother and I have been talking about how to get my wife and me to the home.

SOCIAL WORKER: It's not only getting there; it's also how to leave the old place.

MR. R., JR.: That should be no problem. I'll come over with the truck, we'll load up, won't we, Dad, and off we are.

MRS. R.: I talked with the nurse and she said we could bring one piece of furniture. She said they prefer residents using what they got there and not cluttering things up too much.

MR. R., JR.: That makes it all easier. Then I won't even need the big truck. I can just put the small trailer at the back of the car.

SOCIAL WORKER: Thinking out loud about leaving the place where you lived for 50 years and where you [looking at Mr. R., Jr.] grew up may make it easier to leave for the last time.

MR. R.: Junior doesn't understand anything. He just talks all the time.

SOCIAL WORKER: Let's talk about the practical things that have to get done first.

The progress of which Carlton speaks in his definition of facilitation may be seen in the fact that it is no longer Mr. R. alone who comes to see the social worker. Both Mrs. R. and the son are now actively involved in planning and considering how to make the move from home to the institution. There are several aspects to be considered, as well as many difficulties in the process. One is the lack of understanding of the emotional meanings of giving up one's home, as expressed by the flippancy of Mr. R., Jr. The other is the antagonistic relationship of father and son. A third is the institutional nurse's reference to the R.'s possessions as "clutter." Nevertheless, by keeping the focus as much as possible on the task at hand, the social worker facilitates movement, such as saying goodbye to the old place, how to arrange the entry into the new home, and involving the three family members in all phases of the move. These matters are the subject and object of social worker and client facilitation. For the latter it is a kind of self-facilitation, and for the social worker it is a facilitative function directed toward the clients. Each plays into the other, so that the work of the helping group is a true membership activity. While it is beset by many issues and painful problems, there is nevertheless a sense of movement and progress toward the realization of a clear goal.

Options Identification

The identification of options is another common social work technique. Consistent with the membership perspective, options identification is not done by the social worker alone. Rather, it is a task for all members of the helping group.

The ongoing experiences of the people in the case vignette that illustrates the various techniques of social work practice make clear what options identification involves. In the case excerpt that follows, Mr. and Mrs. R. have spent their first few days in their new home, a home for the well elderly. Two tasks face them. The first is to establish a routine for themselves that takes into account not only their own wishes but also the fact that they no longer live alone. The second task is to continue to work on the ongoing difficulties they are having with their son. What both tasks have in common is the need to identify the options before they make specific decisions.

SOCIAL WORKER: I am not quite sure about what we ought to work on today. You see, I'm only going to be available to work with you for a limited time because the agency doesn't usually follow clients much beyond the time they move to a home like this one. So, we don't have much time left together.

MR. R.: Well, things are going pretty good so far. Don't you think so? [as he looks to his wife].

MRS. R.: Maybe for you they are [addressing the social worker]. He's got himself some buddies here and now he plays cards all day. I don't like the food. Our room is too small, and the whole place feels like a funeral home. I hate it here. And I am bored stiff.

Social workers who work with clients on issues such as those Mr. and Mrs. R. face have a double task. One is to render aid in the management of the losses clients have sustained. The other is to help them to plan their use of time in their new home. The success of the latter depends on the success of the former. Yet, rather than addressing them sequentially, one works on both simultaneously. The reason is obvious. Both take time, and neither is properly dealt with unless they are viewed as interconnected. Options about the immediate future need to be identified as soon as is feasible in order to prevent a pathological syndrome, such as depression, from gaining the upper hand. At the same time, and for the same reasons, healthy grieving ought to be encouraged. This assumes that the social worker understands the differences between mourning and depression. The example that follows makes the point:

SOCIAL WORKER: So, what you face is having to get used to the new place while you still feel badly about giving up your former home.

(The reference to the old home as the former home should be noted as a reality confrontation.)

MR. R.: You can see that my wife doesn't understand that playing cards takes my mind off that.

MRS. R.: And all the time you just let me sit here.

SOCIAL WORKER: Can we talk about how both of you can plan some of your time when you are together and also plan for some time for each of you?

MR. R.: What do you mean? I don't want to be here any more than she does. All this talking makes me sick. It was a mistake to come, I want us to be on our own; and there is not a damn thing about this place I want. Nobody here cares if we live or die. Being old is just like being thrown to the dogs. I know you want to help us but I can't stand you. I want you to get out of here and just let us rot away in any way we want to. And while you are on your way out, you can tell that stupid son of mine that I don't want to see him or anybody else again—ever.

MRS. R.: You can see how upset he gets. I got to be alone, got to take a walk.

The situation was not helped by the announcement on the part of the social worker that he was about to terminate services because of agency policy. This, no doubt, contributed to Mr. R.'s explosive behavior. Yet, one may see in this case the social worker's use of grieving techniques to help the R.'s deal with the loss of their former home and to help Mr. and Mrs. R. identify their options. It is important, however, not to confuse options identification with decision making. Decisions are made after options have emerged in the client's consciousness.

The work of the social worker and Mr. and Mrs. R. demonstrates the fact that techniques are not single and simple events. They often run together, but nevertheless they can be identified. In addition, nothing the social worker does in this vignette is done alone. He is highly alert to the need of both Mr. and Mrs. R. to be involved at every step in the process. When this involvement is not present, as when the social worker and Mr. R. first considered the R.'s move to the home without the direct involvement of Mrs. R., the social worker handled the situation by making a cognitive and an affective statement: "I feel uncomfortable about your wife not being here. . . ."

Interpretation

Interpretation refers to those social worker efforts to put into words what is implied, latent, and avoided in terms of speech. Of all the major techniques, it is the least participative one, and it depends on the social worker's understanding of subtleties that clients often do not see. The exception is in work with more than one client. The difference is probably determined by the degree of closeness to what is interpreted, because when the interpretation of one's behavior affects oneself, one is more likely to defend oneself against the recognition of the unpalatable than is true in cases involving some distance. Thus it is that clients often interpret the behaviors of other clients.

Interpretation is manifested by stating the meaning of either one particular behavior or of a series of behaviors that form a consistent pattern. At one point in the work, the following exchange took place among Mr. and Mrs. R., Mr. R., Jr. and his wife, Mrs. R., Jr., who has now joined the helping group, and the social worker.

MR. R.: I can't believe that mother and I have been here 7 months. I still don't like the place. And I don't like to see what's happening to her health.

MRS. R.: Don't worry about me. I'll take care of myself and the kids will do what they have to do [she nods to her son and daughter-in-law].

MRS. R., JR.: I can't understand what is going on here. If a stranger would drop in and listen to us, she would think that Junior and the children and I neglect you. The fact is that we do all we can to make you comfortable, spend lots of time and even money to let you know we love you. I know Junior is not always the most tactful person, but he goes out of his way to please you. All he gets from you, Dad, are insults. I know that I am only the daughter-in-law and should keep my mouth shut, but it's time somebody said it.

SOCIAL WORKER: All of us really fear the same thing. As the years go by we all fear that we will lose our independence and control over things. That is what you are concerned about [looks at the parents] and it is exactly the same thing that worries you [looks at Mr. and Mrs. R., Jr.] first for your parents and then for yourselves. You are right; it is scary. As I see it, that is what the yelling and all the accusations really mean.

MR. R.: You've got a point there.

Mr. R's last remark confirms his understanding and acceptance of the interpretation. He, in effect, participates in it by responding to it. The point, however, is less that he accepts it than that he deals with it. Had he rejected it, the conclusion would be the same; it would still be his way of conducting his membership. The social worker, however, would have faced a different set of intervention issues if Mr. R. had rejected the interpretation. What is not evident in this excerpt is how the other clients reacted.

It should be clear from these examples, all taken from a single helping group, that the series of techniques illustrated in them are replicable in all other kinds of helping groups; that there is a sense of universality about them; and that they depend upon the membership behaviors of all participants, whatever these behaviors may be. This vignette also illustrates an instance where the social worker makes a mistake: the somewhat disconnected announcement about his agency's policy of not following clients and his consequent need to terminate with the R's. This too, however, is membership, the impact of which Mr. R. acted out in his angry response to the social worker. Thus, this excerpt makes clear the fact that only in very rare instances does any technique or behavior affect only one person. Instead, even when each person emerges distinctly in terms of the kind of person he or she is, it is always as a member of something beyond him or her that animates the social work process. In part, this has to do with social work technique, but it also has to do with a more subtle, attitudinal dimension of the social worker's approach. From the outset, the social worker steers his participation in the direction of considering not only those present in the helping group but also those who are not; that is, he works in a social mode. He comments on the absence of Mrs. R. specifically, in one instance. In others, when he talks only with Mr. R., his references are to Mrs. R., his son, and his son's family. Thus, what began as work with one client progressed to work with four clients in the latter stages of the vignette.

It will be noted that the troubles the R. family faces are fairly common and that their ways of dealing with them have all the earmarks of the everyday behavior of millions of others. Fear, anger, competition, emotional outbursts, and also thoughtfulness and caring are the common ways in which members behave. There is nothing esoteric here. The problems at hand reflect the common human condition, helped and addressed by another human being who is knowledgeable about what he is doing.

Clarification, confrontation, interpretation, options identification, counseling, facilitation, and many others are generic techniques of all social work. It matters little what the presenting problem is. Certainly, the clients do not distinguish between mental health, family, corrections, and health problems. This does not mean that social work should not have specializations, but rather that *methodological* specialization is unnecessary and redundant. Indeed, it should be noticed that in the R. case the social worker makes a smooth transition from work with one client to work with four. There was no noticeable change here from a "now I do casework" stance to "now I do group work" or to "now I do family work." People came into the work as they needed and wanted to.

This perspective on practice leads to a much needed demystification of the so-called clinical social work process. In fact, whatever it is that the social worker does, he or she does it in slightly modified ways whatever the setting and whatever the client's purposes might be. Much the same can be said about the artificial distinctions made between clinical social work and community social work. The content of the work may differ, but the technical resources the social worker uses are much more similar than is generally assumed. The detailed analysis of the interaction process of a committee meeting, for example, reveals practically the same behaviors by both committee members and the social worker member as does a clinical social work record. Failure to understand the unity of the profession divides it and keeps it divided, with the result being that social work still lacks the autonomy needed to be a freestanding profession.

SOCIAL WORK INTERVENTION AND CULTURAL MEMBERSHIP

It is very easy, and in fact likely, that social workers, like other people, tend to be unaware of their assumptions about the norms and values that guide their clients' and their own behavior. The conflict between Mr. R. and Mr. R., Jr. is a good example. It can have a wide variety of meanings, depending on the values the participants and observers hold to be important. Some may see the conflict as a chronic, disabling condition of family life. Others may see it as normal interchange between father and son, giving the matter no more than passing attention. Still others might think that the social worker ought to articulate his or her observations of it and invite the two men to find some kind of solution for it.

Lum (1986) has addressed the issue of working with minority group members, not merely understanding them. Lum's focus is on the social worker's activities, on what he or she actually says, communicates without words, and assumes to know about client values and norms. One of Lum's interests is the social worker's self-disclosure. His main point is that with some minorities of color, the social worker's self-disclosure forms the basis for trust between clients and the "stranger from the outside," namely the social worker. In this connection, he makes the following "task" recommendations:

Practice professionals [should] self-disclose with a minority client in an initial session. Do not wait to begin with the problem. Initiate the conversation and allow the client to get to know you as a person. Introduce yourself, sharing your background and some information about your work at the agency. Personalize the relationship to the extent that the client finds out about an interesting facet of your life. Find a common ground for conversation with the client so that it can serve as a bridge between you. (p. 105)

Although these prescriptions may appear to be somewhat global and therefore overdetermined, their value lies in the fact that they address the social worker's behavior rather than his or her intellect alone. Lum speaks much less of values and attitudes than of action. One might add that the cultural characteristics of minority (and majority) group members should be something far more than just respected. They should be reflected in the social worker's intervention. Lum specifically sets down his conception of the social worker role and moves it directly, openly, and specifically from the tradition of neutrality, within which most of social work has evolved, to one of self-disclosure in the interest of engaging the client. The social worker does not remain an unreachable stranger, but is an identified and identifiable human being who, while respecting boundaries, avoids entering the membership of the helping group as a psychosocial neuter. All the safeguards of the conscious use of self (emotional, ethical, and intellectual) are present, yet they do not serve as prohibiting factors, but as factors that enable the helping effort in the helping group. This, too, is fundamental to the membership perspective.

Membership, however, does not necessarily mean closeness, intimacy, and a single style of self-disclosure. Lum, for example, points out that caution is needed in what he calls "cultural study" (pp. 106–108). He cites Kahn and his associates' (1975) work with Native Americans to underline the idea:

> In summary, some factors which we consider to be important in providing psychotherapy for the Papago are as follows:
>
> 1. Relying on the mental health technicians;
> 2. Using a crisis intervention approach;
> 3. Avoiding eye contact;
> 4. Approaching therapeutic topics slowly and cautiously;
> 5. Avoiding confrontations;
> 6. Making interpretations very clear;
> 7. Utilizing directive techniques;
> 8. Remaining flexible in regard to time; and
> 9. Talking less than usual. (cited in Lum, p. 108)

Here, too, we see certain prescriptive aspects for the management of professional membership, with a heavy emphasis on what the clinician should do as well as not do. Thus, it is clear that the social worker must not only know about the client, but possess the skills necessary to transpose that knowledge into meaningful behavior.

Finally, while it is relatively easy to define considerations to be taken in assessing clients (Carlton, 1984; Falck, 1981), there are considerable dangers in approaches that are too categorical, too rigid, and too universal. Yet universal to all people, without regard to race, color, minority or majority status, geography, or economic condition, is the fact of membership. There is no group life without membership, and there is no life without the group. The issues before every social worker are those that stem from the kinds of memberships clients portray and the ways they carry on their memberships. These questions apply despite the myriad variations that the answers contain. In all cultures, majority and minority, the issue of membership lies at the heart of social work assessment and at the heart of all the social worker thinks, feels, and does.

CONCLUSION

The common work of social worker and client(s) is conceived as the content of the helping group. That content includes the problems or other subject matter clients bring to social workers, techniques of intervention, cultural variations, and considerations that affect both clients and social workers. These are factors that modify the interactions of the members of the helping group in identifiable ways.

The applicability of the principle of conditional accessibility is always exemplified best when the circumstances of membership call for controlled inputs. In the case of the interaction of social worker and client, this is governed by the tasks to be performed. These tasks are to help and be helped. From the social worker's point of view, what is said, how it is said, and how it is intended to be heard are the determinants of the professional person's behavior and thus illustrate at a relatively high level of visibility a principle of membership that in a more extended and general sense governs most human interaction.

REFERENCES

Carlton, T.O. (1984). *Clinical social work in health settings: A guide to professional practice with exemplars.* New York: Springer Publishing Company.

Falck, H.S. (1981). *The social status examination in health care.* Richmond, VA: Virginia Commonwealth University School of Social Work.

Kahn, M.W., Williams, C., Galvez, E., Lejero, L., Conrad, R., & Goldstein, G. (1975). The Papago psychology service: A community mental health program of an American Indian reservation. *American Journal of Community Psychology, 3,* 88–90.

Keefe, T. (1976). Empathy: The critical skill. *Social Work, 21* (1), 10–13.

Lum, D. (1986). *Social work practice and people of color: A process-stage approach.* Monterey, CA: Brooks/Cole.

7   The Social Worker and the Client II

The advantage in listing social work interventions in terms of techniques can be found in their concreteness. Social worker behavior is observable and replicable. Once one has defined a technique and specified its desired effects, one may develop a potentially unlimited number of ways to apply it. However, other considerations must be taken into account, both prior to and during the use of certain techniques, no matter how specific. Technique is useful only when it rests on the ongoing assessment each social worker (and to a large extent each client) makes of what is taking place in the helping group. Thus, intervention techniques are responses to something other than themselves and have no independent existence.

THE JOINT ASSESSMENT OF CLIENT BEHAVIOR

One knows whether a technique is useful when two conditions are present. The first is the assessment of the client and his or her situation; the second is the monitored process of the helping group itself as it affects each and all of its members. The general, overall assessment of the problem brought to the social worker by the client(s) is indispensible to all forms of social work.

Systematic Assessment

Assessment can be done in systematic fashion. It serves as a general as well as specific guide to social work intervention. In the membership perspective, assessment is done by the social worker and the client *together,* while each plays his or her role. Monitoring is the technique that enables the practitioner to keep track of what is similar and different from the beginning assessment through all phases of the work as the helping process unfolds. Thus, assessment and monitoring are two interlocking activities that occur over time, from the first moment of contact between social worker and client(s) to the last and, in memory, beyond it.

As would be expected, assessment in its most formal sense is largely the preoccupation of the initial stage of social worker–client contact. One hurries to add, however, that assessment making is not a very sophisticated science. It is subject to error and, therefore, also to correction. Every assessment must be viewed as a temporary statement, subject to change through monitoring. As the client's behaviors change, whether for better or for worse, the assessment is revised on the basis of observed data not available at an earlier stage in the common work.

Even if the tentativeness with which assessment making is endowed is a matter of prudence and good judgment, it is also true that the picture of the client that emerges from assessment is not subject to as much variation as one might think. In other words, while a certain conservatism is dictated by the absence of reliable diagnostic categories, it is also true that a skilled social worker takes reasonable chances in the making of assessments. This chance taking is a fundamental condition for intervention. What saves the social worker and the client from the most blatant misjudgments and errors is the response of the client to the social worker's interventions.

In other words, the client's behavior in response to the social worker's behaviors is in the nature of feedback. Thus the social worker, who monitors the social worker–client interaction, obtains more or less immediate information about what works and what does not. Yet even here one must use care, since certain clients give little, and sometimes no, usable feedback or delay it, possibly for days, weeks, or months.

Methods of Assessment Making

There are certain general areas for assessment making with clients that can be named and defined. None are of equal value for all clients and all situations. One assesses those areas of the client's life that are to be addressed by the social worker and the client in order to render and to receive the aid needed. In other words, assessing and monitoring are of value only to the extent that they are necessary and useful for the task that lies ahead. The rule, therefore, is that it is inappropriate and unethical to seek information that is not needed. When one is unclear about the assessment that one needs, it is not uncommon to try out several approaches to determine what it is the client is presenting, what it means, and how it is combined with an estimate of one's own potential helpfulness and with the kinds of services one's agency is prepared to offer the client.

The social worker must be careful to avoid the temptation to try to replicate the medical situation in which diagnosis making is not only of fundamental importance but also implies a certain expertise that the patient does not possess. Social work is not totally free from this temptation because professional social workers do have expertise and specialized knowledge that clients often do not possess. Were this not the case, there would also be no reason to seek out the services of the social worker. One of the areas of expertise the social worker has that physicians rarely have is the ability to involve the client in the assessment of his or her own situation. Social workers make client involvement a central focus from the outset.

The focus in making a social work assessment rests on the client rather than on the questions the social worker asks. In fact, the membership perspective discourages itemized questions, since the aim is not to get answers but to know the client. The assumption is that what the client shares is himself or herself at that moment. Thus, the social worker distinguishes between information as such and the client who supplies it. The preferred way of interviewing in social work is to ask no questions, or very few, and to conduct a conversation in which both client and social worker participate knowingly. For example:

SOCIAL WORKER: In order to get started, it might be a good idea for you to tell me what brought you here. That will give us a chance to begin our work together.

CLIENT: What do you want to know?
SOCIAL WORKER: Anything you think will get our work together started.
CLIENT: I have lots of troubles and I want you to tell me what to do about my wife's drinking.
SOCIAL WORKER: We'll work on it together.

The point is, of course, that not only does the social worker set the rules ("We'll work on it together") but also obtains from the client some idea (extended as the conversation continues) about the latter's current approach to his request for help. It should be noted, for example, that the client assumes that it is he who should do something about his wife's drinking.

It is fairly common that this kind of conversation does not always produce all the material the social worker needs or wants before it emerges spontaneously. Should this be the case, the social worker can simply tell the client that more is needed, say why it is needed, and then ask a question or two.

SOCIAL WORKER: We have been talking for about an hour and have only a few minutes left. In order to schedule my time and yours, I need to know when you can come for appointments. What kind of work do you do and what are your hours?

OR

SOCIAL WORKER: You mentioned your wife but we didn't get to talk about the others in your house. We should think about whether you should come here by yourself. Sometimes it is a good idea to consider meeting with other family members, too, but, of course, that is your decision to make.
CLIENT: Well, we have three daughters. Two are gone and have their own families. The youngest lives with my wife and me.

Two of the main objectives of this approach to assessment making are that the client feels involved in the process and leaves with the impression that not only did he or she give information, but also that something was given in return. Thus, assessment making is a form of intervention. The following example illustrates this idea:

SOCIAL WORKER: We must stop in a few minutes, and I suggest that you and I take a moment to talk about where we are, especially since this is our first time together.

CLIENT: O.K.
SOCIAL WORKER: [waits]
CLIENT: I guess I told you a lot about me. [Silence]
SOCIAL WORKER: I want to let what you told me sink in.
CLIENT: It was the first time anybody really listened to me.
SOCIAL WORKER: You are saying that you feel that you are not used to that.
CLIENT: When did you say you want me to come in again?
SOCIAL WORKER: How are Mondays at five in the afternoon?
CLIENT: Fine with me.
SOCIAL WORKER: [stands up] See you then.

The social worker not only follows up on information after telling the client what it is he or she wants to know and why, but also monitors the process. One should note, for example, that despite the fact that in a first session the client might give evidence of being slightly intimidated, and that he asks to be told how to act, this is material to be kept track of in order to see how it might help or hinder the helping process later. The point is that all client behavior has the potential of contributing to an overall assessment of the client by the social worker.

Were one to repeat the example just given in a community social work situation, one might find the following interchange:

SOCIAL WORKER: We have met for an hour now. Before we stop for today, let's take a few minutes to see where we are.
COMMITTEE MEMBER A: I think we did a lot of work today, but I am not quite clear where all this is going to take us.
SOCIAL WORKER: [waits and looks around]
COMMITTEE MEMBER B: We have some data but I don't know what we ought to do with them.
COMMITTEE MEMBER C: Mary [the social worker] will tell us what to do with them next time—I hope.
SOCIAL WORKER: I think that my role ought to be to get you the data and other information. What we should do with them is something we should work on together.

As in the previous example, this social worker is actively involved in the group process. That is, the social worker gains information and at the same time lets the members of the committee know what his or her role is. The participants give of themselves and take away impressions, information, and a sense of the social worker's competence in working with them.

As long as the social worker guides the work so that the purposes of the helping group are met, it makes relatively little difference where he or she begins. The question is always, "What is it both client(s) and social worker need at the time?" In a first or second session one assumes that both need a chance to get to know each other. What they do not need is to check off a list of questions prepared ahead of time and asked in a routine fashion. That places the stress on the questions and excessive weight on the client ("I have to know her before I can do much for her"). The membership perspective requires a joint emphasis on both (i.e., on what is taking place between social worker and client). This is the main reason why the social worker tells the client what he or she is doing and why.

There is a by-product to the kind of assessment making in the membership perspective; it teaches the client what clientship entails by letting the client know how the social worker perceives the client role. The implication is that one cannot take for granted that clients without previous experience know how to get the most out of their work with the social worker. By letting the client know what the social worker is doing at each step of the initial assessment phase, the client learns what to expect on the basis of his or her own ongoing experience with the social worker.

Thus far the membership approach to assessment making has been discussed in terms of the constancy of the assessment process. This constancy is maintained through use of the technique of monitoring. Emphasis has been on assessment at the beginning of the entire helping process, at the beginning of each session, and at the end of each session. Case excerpts were used to illustrate a first assessment during a first session. Similarly, a case excerpt illustrated how a session is ended (e.g., "where we came from; where we are now"). What remains to be illustrated is assessment of an intermediate session, one that can occur at any point along the continuum of the helping process, and assessment at the end of the entire undertaking. The following excerpt illustrates an intermediate assessment:

> CLIENT: I feel that most of the work I do takes place between appointments.
> SOCIAL WORKER: Hours don't end when you leave here.

CLIENT: I sometimes can't sleep after I've been here earlier in the day.
SOCIAL WORKER: Coming here isn't always pleasant.
CLIENT: I don't feel bad—usually—when I am here with you; it's after I leave here.

OR

CLIENT: I was just thinking the other day that I have been coming here for 9 weeks, and I wonder what good it does me.
SOCIAL WORKER: You sound like a customer, and you want me to convince you that I sell you decent merchandise.
CLIENT: I don't want you to do anything at all. I make my own decisions. When I don't want you anymore, you'll know it—I just won't come back, you [expletive].
SOCIAL WORKER: Let's talk about the way you handle your anger. . . .
CLIENT: I'm not angry, just disgusted.
SOCIAL WORKER: Disgusted with whom or what?
CLIENT: Myself.

OR

SOCIAL WORKER: I suggest that we begin with thinking about what we remember from last week's session.
CLIENT: We talked about my wife's alcoholism.
SOCIAL WORKER: I seem to remember that we also talked about the way you feel about her drinking.
CLIENT: Same thing.

Despite the client's comment at the end of this excerpt, the client's and the social worker's recollections are, of course, not the "same thing." The social worker purposely did not label the wife's reported drinking as alcoholism. The client reports that he remembers talking about his wife, while the social worker remembers talking about the client's feelings about his wife. The point here is that assessment operates constantly during the helping process: The client's perceptions are monitored while the worker simultaneously intervenes by clarification of facts, for example.

Without overstating the importance of identifying the stages and phases of helping, there are certain aspects of the process that are more likely to occur sometime after the beginning of the helping process and prior to the termination. Again, this should not be overstated, especially since one may make a cogent argument for the idea that termination begins with goal-setting and contract-making at the very outset. For example:

SOCIAL WORKER: O.K., I have the impression that we have some idea now about what you want to get out of this.

CLIENT: I think that is right, and 6 weeks from now I might feel better.

SOCIAL WORKER: I hope you will; in the meantime you and I can keep track of how we are doing.

It is easy to see how the social worker and the client build the termination of the helping process into the beginning. This is a particular advantage of contracting: It makes it possible to define an explicit goal. That this goal is subject to revision has already been pointed out in the discussion of assessment making. Revision is always present as an option for both social worker and client members.

Assessment at the end of the helping process follows, in principle, the same pattern noted in the excerpts above. It is, however, important to keep two additional dimensions in mind when the process is ending. One is the termination of the helping relationship; the other is evaluation of the usefulness of the effort that is coming to an end. Particularly in social work practice with clients who are seen for months and sometimes years, attention to termination needs to be direct and focused. Such relationships involve much feeling and dependency, and cannot be resolved precipitously without potentially negative consequences. Much more is involved in termination than merely selecting a date to end and keeping it. When it comes to evaluation of the work done together, it is possible to be more specific and at the same time illustrate how termination and evaluation can work together.

The following excerpt is taken from the final (termination) session of a long-term helping group.

SOCIAL WORKER: We have been talking off and on for several weeks about this being our last session. . . .

CLIENT: I wonder what I'll do with the time. . . .

SOCIAL WORKER: And the time and money you've spent coming here.

CLIENT: I'll be rich again [laughs].

SOCIAL WORKER: I think that if we can talk about what we have achieved here, you may also get some idea about what you still have to do after we have ended our work. It may also tell us something about what we didn't achieve.

CLIENT: I can't think of that right now. What I remember is coming here the first time and being scared.

SOCIAL WORKER: And now?

CLIENT: I still get scared sometimes when I hear myself talk about my parents. You know, I was brought up to believe that you should *never* criticize your mother and father in front of strangers. I see that differently now.

SOCIAL WORKER: Meaning?

CLIENT: I learned that feelings are feelings and you can't keep hitting yourself over the head just because you have them.

The next excerpt is an example of termination in a short-term helping group where the agenda and the total number of sessions were set at the very beginning. It will be noted that the process of assessment and evaluation is, in principle, essentially the same in the short-term helping group as in the long-term helping group.

SOCIAL WORKER: Today is our eighth and final session together.

CLIENT: I know. It's amazing how quickly they went by.

SOCIAL WORKER: The point is, did you get what you wanted from them?

CLIENT: I think I did. After all, I remember that we said at the very beginning that this was to be a short-time trip. I wanted to figure out whether to break the engagement to Mike and I did.

SOCIAL WORKER: Did break it?

CLIENT: No, figure out whether or not I wanted to.

SOCIAL WORKER: So, the important thing was not whether to break it, but whether you could if you wanted to.

CLIENT: Right—whether timid me could make scary decisions.

SOCIAL WORKER: You still seem to feel a bit scared.

CLIENT: Yeah, but much less than I used to.

In principle, the process here is the same process as in the long-term situation. What is missing in the short-term excerpt is the focus on the relationship of the social worker and client and the symbolic internalization that typically accompanies long-term interventions. However, the manner in which the assessment works its way through the helping process, from the outset to the end (the purpose of the work or the manner in which it occurs), can be seen in both excerpts.

Assessment is one of the universals in all self-conscious, focused, and purposeful social work.

What has been illustrated in all of these excerpts are the qualitative aspects of membership, the ways in which persons are members of common situations. In all instances these members were clients and social workers. They illustrate how the interactional process varies according to (1) the task at hand; (2) the clients and the social workers involved; (3) work done in previous sessions, with the exception of first sessions; and (4) how both clients and social workers perceive their relationships. Assessment through monitoring underlines the dynamic character of social work intervention, provided the clients are actively involved in every aspect of the work.

Assessment Topics

To bring this section to an end, some of the topics that are typically subject to assessment in social work are briefly identified. None apply to all clients all of the time. The purpose in listing them is to consider the varieties of concern that social workers need to demonstrate in their work with clients. Nor is there any intent to suggest that any one is more relevant than others; their relevancy depends on what the client wants or needs and what social workers can provide.

There are a number of standard areas for the development of social work assessments. Since they need to be useful for a wide variety of social work interventions, they are conceptualized at a fairly high level of generalization. The intent is not that the social worker alone use them by reformulating them into questions asked of clients. Rather, they are to be employed as subjects of conversation that involve the client and the social worker jointly.

In the first formulation of assessment making in the membership perspective (Carlton, 1984; Falck, 1981), 15 assessment dimensions were developed for health social work. Thus, while they were focused on one specialization in social work, they are general enough so that with modification they are applicable to many other areas of social work practice as well. Even if one were to develop a single set of assessment dimensions for all of social work, their specific use would still be justified only to the extent that they were adjusted to the situation(s) of the particular clients with whom one works at a given time. The assessment items that follow are derived from the earlier formulations noted above.

Life Stage

To what developmental stage in life does the client(s) belong? What developmental stage has the client achieved?

Condition for which Social Work Help is Sought

What is the client's stated need or problem?

Family and Other Memberships

What family and other membership issues are linked to the situation for which help is sought, and how are they linked?

Racial/Ethnic Membership

Is the client a member of a racial or ethnic group? Do cultural factors influence the social management of the situation or problem for which help is sought?

Social Class

Estimate the social class membership of the client(s) and its connection with the social management of the situation, problem, or condition.

Occupation

How does the situation, condition, or problem influence the client's occupation, that is, abilities/disabilities as well as temporary/permanent limits on work functioning?

Financial Condition

How does the client's situation, condition, or problem influence his/her financial condition? What income maintenance efforts are being made? Does the client have savings? Is the client supported by others? By whom?

Entitlements

Does the client carry health, accident, disability, life insurance? Is it being used to pay for services being sought? Who pays? Is the client entitled to veterans' benefits?

Transportation

What transportation is available to the client? To relatives, friends, and others with whom the client wants and needs contact?

Housing

What kind of housing is available? What is the impact of the client's situation, condition, or problem on housing, or housing on the management of the situation? Who lives with the client?

Mental Functioning

Describe the client's mental functioning. Is the client aware of time, place, or person? Can the client participate knowledgeably in decision making in regard to his/her future?

Cognition

Does the client understand the nature of his/her situation, condition, or problem? How does the client express concern over the condition?

Compliance (when appropriate)

Can the client follow medication and other self-care instructions? Who can assist clients in this regard? Upon whom is the client dependent?

Psychosocial Elements

How ready or reluctant is the client in asking for help? Or in using it when offered? How does the client work with the social worker or other help-giving people?

Metaphysical Beliefs

What kinds of metaphysical beliefs does the client hold? How does the client explain to himself or herself the meanings of misfortune, death, disease, injury, and responsibility? How do these meanings manifest themselves in the behavior of the client(s)?

It should be noted that although the assessment items listed address general social work issues, they can be modified as needed for use in particular social work specializations. The intention is to illustrate the types of assessment categories that the membership perspective requires. It should also be clear that the items heavily favor membership issues, issues that are constantly illustrated by the investments people make in the meanings that the behavior of any given person has for others.

CONCLUSION

Assessment making in the membership perspective of social work can be performed systematically, with the full involvement of the client(s). Techniques and dimensions of assessment making can be identified in operational form and varied according to needs of the client and social worker members in the helping group. Reasonably standardized assessment items have been identified and are usable with some situational changes in a wide variety of social work efforts.

REFERENCES

Carlton, T.O. (1984). *Clinical social work in health settings: A guide to professional practice with exemplars.* New York: Springer Publishing Company.

Falck, H.S. (1981). *The social status examination in health care.* Richmond, VA: Virginia Commonwealth University School of Social Work.

8 Community Social Work in the Membership Perspective

Community social work *is* social work and, as are other social work methods, subject to analysis and understanding through the lens of membership. The four dimensions of membership—social interaction, symbolization, internalization, and biological behavior—apply to community social work as they do to all other forms of practice.

Attention in this chapter is directed to the following: general considerations about community social work; interactional dimensions of community social work; symbolization in community social work; internalization in community social work; the goals of community social work; motivations and perceptions of community social work; the context of community social work; community social workers, other social workers, and other professionals in community social work; and the religious impulse and community social work. This is a formidable list of topics. The overall task is to demonstrate how and why community social work may be thought of as rendering professional aid in the management of membership.

GENERAL CONSIDERATIONS ABOUT
COMMUNITY SOCIAL WORK

Community social work is defined as those social work activities that address community issues on a broad level and in diverse ways. What these diversities have in common is that both the problems and their consequences are of profound importance. The administration of a single social agency, or of a state department of social welfare, or the raising of funds in a given community, may in and of itself suggest limited concerns and involvement by people interested in such work. However, social welfare, at times referred to as a service industry, is of such size and proportion in relation to the Gross National Product that its management influences the lives of millions, for example, financial contributors, recipients of help, taxpayers, professionals, volunteers. In addition, public social welfare is a political issue of major complexity with multiple and conflicting motivations, forms, financing, and ideologies. In the private sector, if one can assume that there exist sharp differences between public and private social welfare, the political processes are only slightly evident, but as every experienced social worker knows, they are hardly less complex. While it has been extraordinarily difficult to reduce all of the diverse efforts and interests represented in the social welfare enterprise to a single common denominator, that part of social work most directly concerned with these matters is labeled community social work. One is fully aware of the limitations of the term and the many community and national concerns and functions that it accommodates only in part.

One of the attributes of community social work, as compared to clinical social work, is that it has no *direct* client. Insofar as particular persons are affected by the decisions made and business conducted by community social workers, they are of secondary importance. A bank president sitting on the board of directors of a United Fund is not the personal client of social workers who staff the agency, nor is the priest who serves on a neighborhood committee concerned with public housing a personal social work client. The primary focus of community social work is the community and its representatives.

Aside from these major differences in the perception and definition of the clientele, the number of community social workers is very much smaller when compared to clinicians. Clinicians by far out-number community social workers. For many clinical social workers, community social work is somewhat akin in status to the "environment" (Strean, 1985). In fact, many clinical social workers acknowledge that community social work is an integral component of social work almost as an afterthought. And, indeed, community social work appears to be of interest to dwindling numbers of social workers and students. It is important not to dismiss this fact as some unfortunate accident of history or as some unexplainable development that could not have been foreseen. Nearly two decades ago Gurin (1970) reflected concern about this state of affairs in a detailed examination of community organization practice. In pointing out the multifariousness of such practice, he suggested that it ought to be interdisciplinary in its approach and that schools of social work ought to employ non-social workers to teach it. Yet, there is little indica-tion that a body of knowledge and practice peculiar to this kind of practice exists.

A further problem of community social work practice in all its forms is that it, like clinical social work, has been caught up in the individual–environment distinction. Individual work is left to the clini-cians, while community social workers tend to think of themselves as working with "the (social) environment." Were the lack of theoretical definitions of community social work such that these distinctions merely portrayed an academic exercise with unknown or unimportant conse-quences, one might ignore them. Community social workers, however, are needed to address those national issues and problems that will not yield to solution by reference to environments. Work with minorities also requires community social workers. In light of the comments about work with minorities in Chapter 6, it is important to note that such groups are far less interested in the individualism of the predominant culture than with peoplehood and community. Mexican-Americans and Chicanos are two examples of such groups. As Gibson (1983) notes, less rigid social work models are needed in order to take into account the requirements of these communities. Despite the fact that these are groups that grow in size more rapidly than others and that they are marked by economic poverty, there has been to date no theoretical step forward in social work that adequately takes into account people-hood and community as basic to work with people, be they minority or majority group members.

Even though no major theory exists for community social work that comes even close to the richness and expansiveness of clinical social work theory, many social workers "graduate" into administrative, policy-making, planning, and other roles that come under the rubric of community social work. Usually their graduation is less a matter of education or career planning than it is a natural consequence of "moving up" in the profession.

Despite the unwieldiness of community social work and despite the absence of a cohesive, clear conceptualization of its practice, it is necessary to attend to this dimension of social work from a practical standpoint. On this level, there are a number of observations that have direct practical implications. The first is that the membership perspective is as applicable to community social work as it is for any other component of the profession, provided its basic assumptions are carefully explicated and examined. It is the purpose of this chapter, therefore, to demonstrate why the current overdrawn distinctions between clinical and community social work are unnecessary and how all of social work can be thought of as one profession within a single conceptual framework.

INTERACTIONAL DIMENSIONS OF COMMUNITY SOCIAL WORK

Two crucial aspects of community social work are the ability to lead other members of groups and the abilty to interact with them. Since the membership perspective also defines the staff of the social agency as a group, these abilities are not confined to committees and similar groups. The agency, as a group, includes everyone from the executive director to the secretary, the professional staff, and the nonprofessional staff (i.e., all those people who in some way contribute to the total effort of the agency to fulfill its social purpose). In clinical settings, this definition includes the clients as well. In community agencies, it includes volunteers.

Thus defined in membership terms, the community social worker is able to draw on understanding of group dynamics and on the findings of a large number of research studies on small groups. In drawing on these research findings, however, the social worker must be cautious and sensitive to problems posed by inadequate research methodology that tends to build in reductionism and to characterize groups as if they were individuals who behave. Nevertheless, there are benefits to be derived from these studies, especially those on decision making, which are particularly applicable to community social work.

Interaction studies are a basic science component of the membership perspective. By viewing the ability to interact with others as the operational definition that characterizes the member, the door to one of the central needs of any community social work effort is opened. That is, social workers need to have substantive knowledge of subject matter pertinent to the tasks of the group and of group process and group dynamics sufficient for the worker to positively influence the other group members. In other words, the skill of the social worker in either chairing group meetings or helping others do so (lay chairs of committees, presidents of boards of directors) helps the entire membership meet their common objective.

This skill presupposes professional knowledge, expertise, and leadership behavior. However, this is by itself sufficient only to the degree that it is accompanied by knowledge about those members who do not hold office but are vital to the success of the undertaking at hand. In community social work this entire catalogue of necessary skills, the ability to influence others effectively, to compromise without relinquishing basic positions, to select (elect) officers and chairs of subgroups, to prevent groups from splitting into too many subgroups that hinder the work, is basic to community social work practice.

Leadership

Ross and Hendry (1957) pointed out that leadership theory need not rest exclusively on understanding charismatic or trait theories of leadership, or even on the function of one individual who is named "the leader." They suggested instead that there are three types of leaders. The first is "the person who has achieved pre-eminence by unique attainment, who is *ahead* of his group, a person of the caliber of Einstein." The second is "the person who by designation, for whatever reason, has been given official leadership status involving formal authority, who is *the head* of his group." The third is "the person who emerges in a given situation as capable of helping the group determine and achieve its objectives and/or maintain and strengthen the group itself, who is *a head* of his group" (p. 15).

For the membership perspective, as it was for Ross and Hendry, the major interest lies in Types 2 and 3 and how they manifest themselves in the membership group. In connection with Type 2 leadership, the management of group conflict, as an aspect of decision making, can pose serious problems for the social worker. One way of using the potential of group conflict is to insist that decision making be truly a group process. This means that the social worker takes care to ensure that decisions affecting the community group's task are actually made in the presence of and with the participation of all the members, rather than by the leader, who might otherwise make decisions informally or in consultation with colleagues and friends, some of whom may not even be members of the group. This is a difficult and largely unexamined problem for the social worker, who is not always informed of the actions of the leader outside the group. In situations where community issues involving money, business connections, and other private concerns about community power and authority are variables, it is especially easy for the leader and one or two others to dictate decisions to the group that is officially or theoretically in charge, thus avoiding potential group conflict. The aim of the social worker when this is the case must be to make the group as fully functional as a membership vehicle as possible and to insist on the inviolability of group process.

Insofar as Type 3 leadership is concerned, leadership is any action that promotes the purposes and goals of the undertaking. Thus, one does not speak of "the leader," but of leadership behavior, with the implicit advantage that each member can, at least potentially, engage in leadership behavior and receive recognition for it. The issue is not whether one form of leadership is better than the other. Rather, it is awareness that leadership expresses itself in many ways and that in community social work in particular there are choices to be made about its definition and exercise.

While there is a great deal of research on leadership (Stogdill, 1974), there are some professional issues peculiar to social work that require comment. One of these has to do with the designation of the social worker in client and in community groups. In the former there exists the tendency to speak of the social worker as the group leader, particularly in treatment groups. As already noted, however, the term treatment implies that social workers treat illness. This problem is compounded when the client is defined as a patient and/or logically reduced to the status of a follower because the social worker has taken for himself or herself the title of leader. Not only does this have serious implications for the social self-determination of clients, but by extension it suggests that the dependency issues so many clients bring to their social workers are fixed. It also subjects them to the double message that professionals alone exercise power while simultaneously suggesting that clients should become more able to engage in decision making affecting their lives away from the social agency and social worker.

In community social work, one rarely hears social workers referred to as leaders of the groups with which they work. The leader is nearly always a lay person who acts as chair of the committee, board, neighborhood, or other group. The social worker's role is difficult to define. Often the social worker's designation is enabler, a term with a history suggesting a person who helps others do their job, either by making information and other data available or by assisting in the management of the group process.

SYMBOLIZATION AND REPRESENTATION IN COMMUNITY SOCIAL WORK

In Chapter 2, symbolization was explored as it applies in social work with clients who seek help with personal problems. The point made in that chapter is that social interaction and symbolization are two inseparable aspects of the membership perspective. The one never takes place without the other. In community social work practice, another form of symbolization must be added. This additional consideration is *the meaning of the concept of representation.*

Since a great deal of community social work takes place in groups, it is important to remember that the community social worker must know a good deal about the dynamics of groups. This is why symbolization is also an aspect of community social work. The questions before the social worker are these: What does representation in groups symbolize? What does it mean? How does it appear? What are the critical issues involved in representation? Symbolization is of importance for the added reason that on the face of it a representative group "looks" like any other group, that is, a number of persons sitting around a table or in some other configuration indistinguishable from many others like them.

Representation is a mechanism employed to overcome the barriers inherent in the fact that one cannot work face-to-face with all those whose interests are, in one way or another, involved in the undertaking. In Chapter 3, the very large group was defined as a tertiary group, characterized by non-face-to-face interaction and by its nonintimate nature. The secondary group, in contrast, was described as being face-to-face and nonintimate. The representative group, in the context of symbolization, is a secondary group. The secondary group represents the members of the tertiary group. Both differ from the primary group in that they are nonintimate, that is, members do not meet to share their private, family, and other personal concerns.

Some years before the question of who represents whom in social welfare activity became a matter of great conflict and confusion, Alexander and McCann (1956) noted that representation is "found in the literature in a broad context that does not make clear its true meaning." In discussing boards and committees, they cited McMillen (1945), Trecker (1950), and Trecker and Trecker (1952) to show that "the term has been variously equated with 'diverse interests', 'difference of viewpoint and diversity of belief', or even in a more general fashion, as 'all the groups or interests that make up the agency'" (p. 49). In response to "the push for 'maximum feasible participation' in the poverty programs" of the 1960s, Alexander (1976) sought to bring the concept of representation up to date. One of his main points was that to be meaningful, representation had to be learned and engaged in planfully.

Representation occurs in the following forms. The first form is *elected* representation. In the elected group, an agenda usually exists that is to be "represented" by the elected delegates. A second form is *categorical* representation. This kind of representation is most often initiated by the social worker on behalf of the social agency or organization. The assumption is that someone who is picked to represent certain population groups can, in fact, speak for them. An example of categorical representation is the clergy of various denominations who might sit on a planning board in order to give voice to the views of the religious groups they represent. A third type of representation is one based on the *assumption* that the personal characteristics of the representative are an accurate sample of the universe he or she supposedly speaks for. This type of representation occurs when someone becomes a group member because she or he is a woman, a Black, a Jew, someone from industry. Representation by assumption occurs for two major reasons. One is a belief that there is no way of determining who really speaks for the large number of supposed constituents, and the second is the belief that there is no way of reporting back in order to assure accountability for actions or votes taken in the name of the masses. The solution lies in the assumption that the representatives really represent.

One of the most crucial aspects of the representative character of secondary community groups is the matter of accountability. Unless the population or organization (for example, a labor union) instructs its delegate and holds him or her explicitly accountable, representation becomes a matter of faith and of chance. When getting along with others becomes more important to the representative group members than speaking for the members they represent, extreme complications arise for meaningful community social work. This is why symbolization in community work needs to be taken into account. Unless the community social worker is consciously aware of the role of symbolization in his or her practice, distortions occur.

While identity is a personal matter, the community social worker must be careful not to confuse personal with clinical concerns while working with the members of community groups. If there is such tendency at work, it must be examined and brought under control. At the same time, to overlook the impact of the personal characteristics of group members on the community social work activity is to blind oneself to influences that largely determine the success or failures of community work. When the community social work group becomes a social club, the results can be disastrous for the realization of the group's genuine task. For the community social worker, the psychosocial issues in this regard require that he or she pay attention to problems of leadership, of authority and submissiveness, and of task initiation and passivity. The aim is to help all members of the community social work group, whether professionals or lay people, accomplish their tasks. Unless the social worker knows how to exercise his or her skills in this regard, leadership and leadership behavior will revert to the most verbal, the most aggressive, and the most willing-to-risk members of the group.

While it is necessary to pay attention to group processes, including symbolization, it is too easy to overplay their importance while ignoring the fact that the content of the work is at least of equal importance. The reasons community groups exist in the first place must never be overlooked. Whether group members get along well or poorly pales by comparison when the work that brings them together in the first place is allowed to suffer, is not done, or is done inadequately. The major reason for the work is to accomplish a community task and not primarily to meet the personal needs of the members, although the latter should not be overlooked as a motivating factor. In other words, although symbolization is a very different matter in clinical as compared to community social work, it is of significance in both.

INTERNALIZATION IN COMMUNITY SOCIAL WORK

The aspect of internalization is a more personal expression of the membership perspective than all other dimensions. Social interaction is public. Symbolization, while performed differently by different persons, nevertheless contains an interpersonal, empirically observable component. Internalization, on the other hand, is each member's way of making relationships his or her own.

Internalization has deep roots in the lives of all people, and it addresses the ways in which a person deals with his/her membership relations. It has a historical basis because its creation and manifestation is cumulative. Internalization begins very early in life. It is multifaceted and addresses a whole variety of issues. One of the major ones it addresses is learning how to deal with persons in authority. The manner in which one carries out the implications of one's own power, authority, and influence is derived from experiences with parents and later with authority figures who are not members of the family, as, for example, teachers. Still later, it is derived from further experiences with employers and other persons upon whom one depends for gratification and punishment. Internalization speaks directly and profoundly to issues of one's basic identity (Assael & Perez, 1985).

It is a thesis of the membership perspective of community social work that the internalized relations between the community actors and their compatriots play a largely ignored role in community decision making, especially when the nature of the decisions made are such that it would not occur to most of the participants that anything is involved in the process that is explainable in terms of psychodynamic factors. Yet the social worker will be relatively effectual or ineffectual in community social work practice depending on his or her ability to adapt to various people of different backgrounds and personal agendas. The more the social worker struggles, often without much awareness, with his or her own unresolved problems of internalized (earlier) relationships that seem to have nothing to do with the work at hand, the more difficult it will be to accomplish the task and the greater the danger that it will fail. This does not mean that internalization of past relationships is the only event or even the most significant of variables to be considered. It does mean, however, that such experiences ought not to be dismissed as irrelevant to the work. Community decision making, social agency administration, social planning, and all those situations that call for the management of authority play a role of some significance, involving as they do the clear definition of tasks and the personal assets as well as the vulnerabilities of those who are involved.

Immediately related to internalized relations is a variable that stems largely from clinical sources. This is the management of transference and countertransference phenomena. The first step the community social worker needs to take in this regard is to view these phenomena as perfectly normal manifestations of personality dynamics. In and of themselves, they are unrelated to mental illness or clinical treatment. They speak to universals in human life, namely that it is perfectly natural to endow one's experiences with people with what one has learned and absorbed from previous ones. Since any current experience needs to be evaluated and acted upon on its own terms, rather than in terms of earlier ones, it is reasonable to assume that the social worker, at work in the present, will find himself or herself at a considerable disadvantage if he or she ignores the distortions that occur when one treats current relationships in terms of past ones. The most prominent proponents of the use of psychoanalytic theory in nontreatment settings belong to the British Tavistock School. The influence of this school of thought has been focused on considerations of the contribution of psychiatry to organizational behavior (Rice, 1969). Social work has remained nearly untouched by it. Yet two examples will make the point:

SOCIAL WORKER: I cannot stand the way the board president brags about how much money he makes. He is so self-referential that nothing can take place without him carrying on at length about what he did to get where he is.

SUPERVISOR: All you are expected to do is to get the work done—and not to ruminate about either his or your personality.

SOCIAL WORKER: I can't stand him. Besides, I didn't become a social worker to cater to the powerful and the rich.

SUPERVISOR: So there it is! You have a hang-up about people with money who brag; and you put it on the president of the board, who may or may not be a saint.

OR

SOCIAL WORKER: So now we finally have a woman on the staff of a fund-raising campaign. I still think women can work rather well in a place where you can nurture whiny clients. Fund-raising is better done by men who know how to deal with businessmen and bankers.

In both cases it may well be assumed that what is at work are certain stereotypical attitudes about the role distribution among men and women. In terms of the first example, it is not altogether uncommon to find social workers from a working-class background who struggle with their own deserved, or undeserved as they sometimes see it, achievements. In the second case, the community social worker uses the situation to protect himself from what he experiences as a psychological threat from assertive female colleagues.

What kinds of internalized attitudes are most helpful as they manifest themselves in the behaviors of professionals? The first is reflected in behavior informed by knowledge of the subject matter to which the agency or the committee, the board of directors, advisory commission, or other community group members are to address themselves. The second is a predisposition to carefully select persons who really and truly represent something in the community that amounts to more than themselves, that is, the awareness that the community membership benefits or suffers from what volunteers and staff do or do not do on their behalf. The third prerequisite is the informed social worker who, having a great deal of insight into his or her proclivities, can bring emotional self-discipline to the job, and who, being clear about what social work in the community is, identifies himself or herself as a social worker, even if some of the people with whom he or she works have their own biases about social work and social workers. Self-knowledge and the ability to work with many people of differing backgrounds and persuasions require as much self-disciplined autonomy on the part of the community social worker as is required of his or her clinical social work colleague.

BIOLOGICAL BEHAVIOR

The biological aspects of behavior are difficult to identify in terms of community social work skill and competence, since most of them are nonvoluntary and nonconscious in expression. Nevertheless, as studies of nonverbal behavior have shown (Hare, 1976; Keefe, 1976), bodily communication by facial expressions and grooming and dressing, as well as certain disease states, link bodily and social interaction into a seamless continuity (Weiner, 1977, 1982). Sexual variables influence both symbolization and internalization, just as they connect with interpersonal behavior in other membership groups (Jacobson, 1971; Kernberg, 1976). Thus, as is also true in clinical social work, any attempt by the community social worker to divide the person into biological, psychological, and social parts, rather than to understand these factors as aspects or components of the person, results in an atomistic logic that cannot be supported on scientific grounds.

THE GOALS OF COMMUNITY SOCIAL WORK

The aims of community social work are based on the belief that community life can be influenced toward the realization of those qualities that are of benefit to most members. Its goal, therefore, is to secure and improve the ways in which men, women, and children live together. Perceived in this way, community social work is not, in the words of Wilensky and Lebeaux (1958), a residual effort by which provisions are made for those members who cannot provide for themselves. Instead, the nature of the community social work is always institutional in the sense that all members of the community provide for all those who are of the community, including themselves, whether the community is of local, state, or national scope. Thus, institutional social work is to be regarded as a self-help process that consists of innumerable components. This view differs from the classical writings of Wilensky and Lebeaux (1958), who were quite specific about individuals, individual needs, and individual help as the ultimate aims of social work (pp. 138–139). In contrast, the membership perspective holds that whatever social services government provides, or fails to provide, it is the community that is the ultimate aim, that is, the citizenry that votes, pays taxes, elects representatives who spend its tax dollars on itself. The concept of membership holds no sympathy for the practice that praises or condemns government while relieving citizens of their responsibilities for what is done in their name.

The consequences of community decision making reach far. They range from the allocation of tax monies for public social services to balancing the federal budget. Such decisions imply the need for planning, fundraising, rational allocation of resources, and the administration of social agencies. Conflict over such matters is a fact of public life; it is both inevitable and desirable. It should be protected and supported by a profession that respects the rights of members to speak for their interests. Quite simply, the management of conflict over the allocation of resources for social welfare is an aspect of the management of membership.

MOTIVATIONS AND PERCEPTIONS
OF COMMUNITY SOCIAL WORK

Why do professional social workers, as well as volunteers, involve themselves in community social work and in community work? Most such people probably harbor a vision of the community they serve. The catalogue of reasons includes the following: religiously inspired motivations; ideals, that is, the wish to contribute to a more just world; pity; guilt; and a sense of responsibility for oneself and others. The reasons may be expressions of law and tradition, for example, Jewish social work, or they may express secular human values. A sense of membership pervades them all.

For social workers and others, a vision of the community in its most benign sense forms the central theme of the work they perform. Community workers, professional or volunteer, typically see a community as a whole. With the exception of members who establish support groups related to a chronic illness, they develop benefits and services they themselves might never use. Yet the tasks they address presuppose that it is right and proper to work for a broader social interest than that which is meaningful to one person alone. A criticism of individualism is implicit in community social work, although it is misleading to exaggerate this idea and its implications beyond a certain point.

As noted in an earlier chapter, much confusion exists about the "social," the "environment," and the "community" within professional social work. One example of this confusion is the reference to work with groups of clients as treatment or personal growth group work, while community social work groups are referred to as task-oriented groups. These are misnomers that confuse social work purposes; they imply that clinical social work is not task-oriented and has nothing to do with the community. Such distinctions (Toseland & Rivas, 1984) suggest that in treatment or growth-oriented groups the personal precedes the social, while in task-oriented groups (committees, boards, commissions) there is a nonpersonal task to be performed that does not benefit the participants personally. In fact, both groups have tasks to perform, one the betterment of memberships on a personal basis, the other the improvement of membership on a communal basis. Both kinds of groups can be said to benefit the personal and the communal memberships of all. This thought is implicit in the membership perspective, which holds that personal services are never individual but are always linked, or can be linked, to the common good.

In addition, it is not unusual for a community social worker to be asked by someone who serves on a community committee about personal services for himself or herself, or for members of his or her family or friends. While the standard expectation in such instances is that the community social worker acts as a finder of resources, the community social worker nevertheless hears a good deal that has no link or connection to the primary communal purposes that bring together the social worker and the other person who asks for personal help. The ability to listen, the ability to monitor the interaction, and the skills needed to understand what is being asked for are all skills as useful to the community social worker as they are to his or her clinical colleagues. Furthermore, personality aspects operate in community social work groups as they do in all groups. The most dramatic examples of how personal interest as well as personality dynamics operate in nonclinical settings have been reported by Janis (1972) and Janis and Mann (1977). Particularly impressive is Janis's discussion of White House decision making in connection with the declarations that led to the conflict in Korea and to the Cuban Missile Crisis. Similar dynamics appear to have operated in the failure to respond to the warnings before the Pearl Harbor attack of December 7, 1941. The point is that whether the work being done is primarily of interest to the community or whether it is mostly for the sake of one person, the distinctions are never absolute. Rather, they are relative and reflect gradations. Personality is not confined to the Freudian couch.

THE CONTEXT OF COMMUNITY SOCIAL WORK: VOLUNTEERS AND PROFESSIONAL SOCIAL WORKERS

A major advantage of the comprehensive membership perspective of the human condition for professional social work is that it is able to accommodate a sufficiently wide variety of practice principles to take into account the entire profession, a profession that is widely distributed in its interests and its functions. Without such a model of sufficiently high abstraction, the profession looks not like a single entity but like a series of competing kingdoms, each with its own traditions and domain. In community social work, where they are many other professions at work in various undertakings, the responsibility of social work is to define not what differentiates it from others, but what is central to social work practice. In community social work this centrality lies in the fact that those who represent the community are, indeed, community clients. One need not be ill to be a client, nor does one have to need help with the resolution of personal problems to be a client. One can be a client simply because one is a member of the community, a member who cares, or a member who employs professionally educated personnel to render help in administering, planning, raising funds, and related work. These activities define members of the community as community clients, and the aim of these undertakings is the same as that of the rest of the profession, that is, to render professional aid in the management of membership. In working primarily with various groups who represent the community, one tremendous value of community social work activities lies in the fact that the community social worker need not guess what is wanted and needed in a given community, or in a whole series of communities. While he or she gains a wide variety of information about broad needs from studies, statistical and otherwise, the social worker's primary resource is the community member who represents many others. In addition, volunteers who are involved in community planning, in advisory and policy making roles, in self-help groups, and in other community activities are direct links between the community as a whole and the social worker who is also a member of the community.

It is a matter of common observation that some volunteers, if not all, tend to follow a more or less prescribed career line. Those who do this ascend to increasingly prestige-tied positions as the years go by. For social workers who work for many years in a given community, it is easy to describe how and why a given person, originally serving as a volunteer, ascended a career ladder associated with increasing power, public visibility, and associated rewards. When the ascent is successful, it is a matter of community pride. On the other hand, when the name of such a community member is associated in the public's perception with failures in community efforts, the consequences of such failures are equally observable. Consider, for example, the experience of a former volunteer who had moved on to an administrative position in a local corporation and had agreed to head a fund-raising campaign for a community project. The project failed for somewhat obscure reasons that were only marginally related to the community member whose name was associated with the campaign. Nevertheless, his reputation clearly suffered. This was not a matter he took lightly. As a result, he totally withdrew from further community participation. In membership terms, however, one cannot undo one's memberships simply by resigning and clearing the field. While the person in question remained an active community member through his corporate business position, he bore nevertheless the stigma of a partially compromised membership. This is a situation few people can overlook with equanimity; it centers on the management of failure.

In this connection, it is interesting to consider the effects of such failures on community social workers. Unless the failure of the community project is a disaster of wide and deep proportions, the professionals involved tend to retain a degree of public anonymity. Usually, social workers know what happened and can assign, knowledgeably, at least some of the blame to the appropriate persons involved in the project. Fundraising, however, is nearly always associated with persons of high prestige in order to promote success. While the professionals are rarely seen by the public in such situations, it is the lay person, the community representative, who bears the burden of failure, or the credit that comes with the success of such community-wide efforts.

Despite the issues of the lay person's visibility and the professional's nonvisibility to the public in community work, the ability of volunteers and professionals to communicate openly and frankly with one another is the key to success. A mutual respect for one another's judgments is necessary. They also must be available to one another. These interactional dimensions make such relationships membership situations, as do their opposites. Whether the people involved are volunteers giving time and energy to community work as unpaid participants or professionals employed as community workers, the basic norms of symbolization and internalization, the ability to engage in group interaction and to use one's physical attributes, and the energies that flow from the synthesis of all of these competencies—these are the variables that determine creative or failed community membership.

Volunteerism in American social welfare is no accident of history. There is no Western society that expresses the idea of volunteerism as directly and as universally as the American one. In large part this is because government plays a more central role in the provision of social welfare services in most other Western democracies than is the case in the United States. In most Western countries, the state acts through its civil service in ways quite foreign to Americans. In these countries, the civil service is a fourth branch of government. When, for example, a German citizen registers a claim for publicly funded social services, he or she interacts with government in a way that suggests that the civil service plays a semi-independent role that allows it to dispense funds as if it were the owner of the resources the citizen wants. For the average American observer, this equation lacks a key element that defines the role of government in the United States, namely that government exists at the pleasure of, and in the form mandated by, its membership, that is, its citizenry. Even though the American citizen suffers the rigidities of official agencies in many instances, the basic attitude is still that government serves the citizen, not the other way around.

Consequently, American citizens can and do band together, as members of society, into the largest and most complicated system of volunteer activity in the world. Probably because the entire effort is taken so much for granted, the remarkable social agreement that lies implicitly buried in efforts ranging all the way from minor, local self-help groups to national organizations representing one major need or another is rarely addressed. At the heart of it, there is no formal social membership contract involving official sanction. It is an informal agreement resting on the wish of Americans to be involved. Financial contributions to many of these arrangements are tax-deductible. Tax-deductibility, however, involves the public purse in that the taxpaying citizenry pays indirectly for what government does not supply directly. It is, therefore, accurate to say that voluntary agencies drawing contributions from voluntary givers are, in one sense, quasi-governmental. This is particularly evident in the 1980s as the national government attempts to reduce tax-supported social services while suggesting that the private sector, which in social welfare is the private social agency with its volunteeers, should take up the slack. What is left unsaid is the fact that much of the saving to government on one end of the financial spectrum is offset by tax-deductibility at the other end.

There is still another membership dimension to America's volunteerism. It is that in voluntary social welfare efforts, sponsorship, control, fundraising, and policy making are local activities, even when social agencies are affiliated with national organizations. It is also true that some are more subject to national control than others, such as the American Red Cross, the Boy Scouts of America, and the Salvation Army. Yet large numbers of local agencies, such as the average family agency, even when accredited by the Family Service Association of America or the Child Welfare League, are local organizations with local decision-making authority regarding budget, mission, personnel, and program.

The membership of United Way agencies consists totally of local citizens. In most American communities, the United Way is the fund-raising and the social planning arm of the voluntary social service enterprise. Yet examination of United Way practices reveals that there is little difference in the way the United Way agencies function and the way the average governmental agency works. Like local governmental agencies, United Funds hold hearings on budget allocations, often prescribe agency programs and planning activities (even while denying that this is the case), and exercise considerable community power. They are, by and large, dominated by business people and upper-middle-class members of any given city or town, as the composition of their boards of directors and budget allocation committees make clear.

Still, the sheer expenditure of energy by thousands, if not hundreds of thousands, of Americans who, without material reward, ring doorbells, sit in endless board and committee meetings, and produce and expend millions of dollars per year for an uncountable number of social services, in order to express their common membership in the community, is impressive. It is not an overstatement to say that the voluntary sector in American social services, even with all of its weaknesses taken into account, constitutes an informal social contract, a contract foreseen and written down in no governmental or constitutional document and in no way mandated by government. Some of it may be assisted by government, as tax deductions for charitable purposes and licensing requirements in child welfare services indicate. In essence, however, the American voluntary system is just that—voluntary. The system is supported financially or not by American citizens as it appears right and appropriate to givers as community members. It is within these broadly defined and described parameters that the community social worker works.

COMMUNITY SOCIAL WORKERS, OTHER SOCIAL WORKERS, AND OTHER PROFESSIONALS IN COMMUNITY WORK

Advertisements in newspapers and professional journals, and the fact that non-social workers hold social work positions in numerous settings, make it clear that social work does not exercise professional control over many positions that social workers think of as centrally theirs. It is not infrequent, for example, for advertisements to indicate that "human relations training" is sufficient qualification for social work positions, thus suggesting that there is nothing distinctive about social work as a profession. At other times, social workers and psychologists are invited to apply for a given position without discrimination or consideration of their unique training.

In community social work, the matter is less clear than it is in clinical social work. In part, this is because social workers themselves often find it difficult to identify what it is about a community work position that indicates it could best be done by social workers rather than by public administrators, attorneys, business administrators, or sociologists. Social workers might think that such positions should be theirs. Often, however, in reality, they are not.

When viewing community work, it is indeed possible to become confused about the difference social workers and others make. It is important, therefore, to identify what it is about social work that distinguishes it from other professions in community work, regardless of "boundary problems" that exist between social work and other groups. The fact that the central social work purpose has not been adequately applied to community social work is undoubtedly a result, at least in part, of the slow development of theory that has characterized community social work practice over the years.

The membership perspective, however, offers practice principles that are as applicable to community social work as they are to work with personal problems. With this applicability in mind, we make the following further observations.

First, both community social work and clinical or personal social work deal with substantive human problems that require solution. In clinical social work, it is the personal problem of a member, or members, that needs social work attention. Social work intervention is focused in such work on those issues and needs related to the way clients want to conduct their lives in relation to themselves and others. In community social work, the intervention has to do with issues that go beyond the needs of any given person, family, or small group of members. Both, however, involve helping people manage their memberships.

Second, both clinical social work and community social work

emphasize the quality of membership, rather than the quantitative aspects of membership alone. The inference is that it is clear that community work is usually a form of group work. Its content may be administrative, program planning, fund-raising, or other activities, yet *its process is that of the small group.* There are exceptions, but this is the dominant trend. It is in this regard, more than in any other—save the need for sophisticated understanding of personality theory and its relatedness to social behavior, especially with regard to decision making in small groups—that social work expertise within the membership perspective makes its greatest contribution to community social work. The methodological essence of community social work is small group activity in the context of administration, planning, fundraising, and allocation.

COMMUNITY SOCIAL WORK
AND THE RELIGIOUS IMPULSE

You shall not subvert the rights of the stranger and the fatherless; you shall not take the widow's garment in pawn; . . . When you reap the harvest in the field and overlook a sheaf in the field, do not turn back to get it; it shall go to the stranger, the fatherless, and the widow. When you gather the grapes of your vineyard, do not pick it over again; that shall go to the stranger, the fatherless and the widow. Always remember that you were a slave in the land of Egypt. (Deuteronomy 24:17–22)

Religious affiliation has powerful membership implications in personal and in community life. In American society, religion and social welfare have had, and still enjoy, a close relationship. Quite aside from theological reasons, it is obvious that religion is a communal, membership-bound effort. In terms of the meanings of social justice, charity, righteousness, and salvation, its expression is necessarily of a group nature. This is the case even for the giver who gives alone, that is, outside of any structured arrangement for the systematic collection of funds, alms, food, or clothes. But religion is prescriptive by its nature and purpose. The above citation, from the Holiness Code in the Book of Deuteronomy, is a fundamental example of the relationship between religion and social welfare because, aside from its prescriptive character, it intones the nature of the human community and the rights and obligations of its members.

To a considerable extent, however, the relationship of religion and social welfare in American life has been characterized by problems and tensions with historical roots. In part, this is also the result of the different ways various denominations view that relationship. Protestantism, as Coughlin (1964) notes, only recently relented on its tendency to work solely through the individual for a more just social order when it recognized the need to become directly involved in social welfare efforts in their institutional forms. Roman Catholicism embraces the concept of subsidiarity, which holds that in the light of certain obligations on the part of the state, it is the obligation of the Church community to fill in, "to enable," as Coughlin describes subsidiarity, the state by providing social services in areas where its functions are either insufficiently discharged by the state or where they would be inappropriate. In regard to Judaism, Coughlin points to the conflict between secular and religious Judaism in the social welfare effort. Secular behavior and religious behavior in Judaism, however, are not nearly as radically distinguished from each other as is the case in some other religious communities. Yet, Coughlin rightly observes that many Jews consider themselves to be loyal Jews without paying much attention to theologico-religious issues. For most Jews the attention is on peoplehood, on the membership concerns of the Jewish community. All in all, the picture of religion and social welfare is a mixed one, encompassing differing motives, goals, and methods as well as beliefs and convictions.

The task at hand, however, is not to detail the role of religion in American social welfare. Rather, it is to examine how community social work employs the religious aspects of the membership perspective. In this regard, as soon as one points to the exigencies of sectarian social agencies, one has also touched upon a community that represents social values that go beyond those of any given social worker. As an employee of a social agency, the social worker is forced to come to terms with value systems more characteristic of tertiary groups (non–face-to-face and nonintimate) than those of the secondary group—the church or the synagogue. The social agency represents tertiary values.

In a public social agency, the concern is not to violate those norms that define purpose, method, and belief. In the sectarian agency, much more than acquiescence is expected; loyalty is required. Loyalty is fundamentally voluntary in character, especially in matters of religious membership and religious conviction. At the same time, even when religiously sponsored social agencies do employ staff of differing religious convictions, and sometimes of none, they prefer to employ persons to serve members of their own communities who need social work help, who are by personal conviction loyal to their ideas and doctrines. In other words, the practical, concrete expression of religious values is more than a matter of principles stated in writing; it also includes the religiously linked messages the social agency gives the clients, plus the loyalties and beliefs of their staffs.

Certain social agencies will not participate in divorce counseling or abortion counseling except under the most strictly and closely defined conditions, and even then do so only hesitantly. Jewish social agencies, even when their services are essentially secular, observe Jewish holidays by closing their doors; and Jewish community centers and homes for the aged serve only kosher food, even when clients do not insist that they do so. The essential point is that community-based values are translated into official behavior, with some degree of expectation that staff at least not violate them while at work and represent them as their own. Membership in community is the central theme, and it expresses itself in many ways. It always plays a role.

Linked to these membership concerns, in this case matters of religious relevance and issues of group loyalty, is the fact that the religious group as a type nearly always implies or otherwise suggests certain standards for the qualitative aspects of membership. These aspects, in other words, indicate how one would know a "good Catholic" or a "good Jew" if one saw one, by defining his or her social behavior.

In Jewish tradition, the answer is linked to social welfare activities in the terms of righteousness (Zedakah) and Gemilut Hasadim. While righteousness is biblically legislated, Spiro (1984) points out that Gemilut Hasadim cannot be made a matter of command since it has to do more with the quality "and the sensitive, compassionate response" to human rights and human needs. Thus, "Gemilut Hasadim may be thought of as the ultimate level of Zedakah, in terms of a continuum or gradation" (p. 450). Spiro's comments are of importance to all religious memberships, especially in connection with social welfare, because they address the qualities of membership and not only its existence. Religion, in the ways best known in the United States, prescribes the membership behavior that is to be judged, and it reflects, therefore, the quality of social welfare behavior. In other words, while secular life may demand certain kinds of membership behavior, simply because all members are members of each other, religion in its own ways comments on the qualities of that life in religious terms. Quality of membership, when linked to religious tradition and precept, expresses itself not only in primary and secondary group terms but reaches into the tertiary group, the community, where religiously expressed values and norms form the metaphysical basis for membership on earth among other members. In this sense, clinical social work with its seeming preoccupation with one or a few members at a time and community social work with its attention to the masses join, in the sense that both ultimately address the same concerns.

CONCLUSION

In this chapter community social work was discussed in light of the membership perspective. The concept of clientship was modified to fit the purposes of community social work and then viewed from a variety of further perspectives. These included the empirical aspects of membership and social interaction and biological behavior, as well as the inferential, nonempirical, yet crucially important dynamics of symbolization and internalization. The goals of community social work and the involvement of social workers, volunteers, and other professionals in community work were also discussed. Finally, the religious impulse in community social work was pointed out. Goals, the involvement of professionals and volunteers, and the role of religion were presented as extensions of the basic four components that define membership: (1) social interaction; (2) biological functioning; (3) symbolization; and (4) internalization.

REFERENCES

Alexander, C.A. (1976). What does a representative represent? *Social Work, 21* (1), 5–9.

Alexander, C.A., & McCann, C. (1956). The concept of representativeness in community organization. *Social Work, 1* (1), 48–52.

Assael, M., & Perez, L. (1985). The lack of national identity: A psychopathogenic factor. *Journal of Psychology and Judaism, 9* (1), 5–16.

Coughlin, B.J. (1964). *Church and state in social welfare.* New York: Columbia University Press.

Gibson, G. (Ed.). (1983). *Our kingdom stands of brittle glass.* Silver Spring, MD: National Association of Social Workers.

Gurin, A. (1970). *Community organization curriculum in graduate social work education: Report and recommendations.* New York: Council on Social Work Education.

Hare, A.P. (1976). *Handbook of small group research.* New York: Free Press.

Jacobson, E. (1971). *Depression.* New York: International Universities Press.

Janis, I.L. (1972). *Victims of groupthink.* Boston: Houghton Mifflin.

Janis, I.L., & Mann, L. (1977). *Decision making.* New York: Free Press.

Keefe, T. (1976). Empathy: The critical skill. *Social Work, 21* (1), 10–13.

Kernberg, O.F. (1976). *Object relations theory and clinical psychoanalysis.* New York: Jason Aronson.

McMillen, W. (1945). *Community organization for social change.* Chicago: University of Chicago Press.

Rice, A.K. (1969). Individual, group, and intergroup processes. *Human Relations, 22* (6), 565–584).

Ross, M.G., & Hendry, C.E. (1957). *New understandings of leadership.* New York: Association Press.

Spiro, J.D. (1984). An exploration of Gemilut Hasadim. *Judaism, 33* (132), 448–457.

Stogdill, R.M. (1974). *Handbook of leadership.* New York: Free Press.

Strean, H.S. (1985). Clinical social work: What's in a name? *NASW News, 30* (8), 17.

Toseland, R.W., & Rivas, R.F. (1984). *An introduction to group work practice.* New York: Macmillan.

Trecker, H.B. (1950). *Group process in administration.* New York: Women's Press.

Trecker, H.B., & Trecker, A.R. (1952). *How to work with groups.* New York: Women's Press.

Weiner, H. (1977). *Psychobiology and human disease.* New York: Elsevier.

Weiner, H. (1982). The prospect for psychosomatic medicine. *Psychosomatic Medicine, 44* (6), 491–517.

Wilensky, H., & Lebeaux, C. (1958). *Industrial society and social welfare.* New York: Russell Sage.

9 The Sense of Community: On the Reciprocity of Membership

ON MEMBERSHIP AND COMMUNITY

The main theme of this book has been to demonstrate that the basic element in social work is to render aid in the management of membership of persons, that is, to help them modify the qualities of their membership with other people. To explore the factual base of this view and its implications for social work practice, the temptation to stray from the main theme and to enter into a more speculative, philosophical mode was avoided.

Thinking and speaking in the language of membership is not a simple task. In fact, it is easy to fall back into the style of individualistic thought and speech, and it takes a good deal of conscious discipline not to do so. The reason is, of course, cultural determinism. That is, the fact of being a member of an individualistically oriented society makes it difficult not to fall into line with its assumptions— the internalized modes drawn from that culture—and to focus on what beliefs, rather than facts, tell us. For persons who need to think that they are unique, separate, totally private, and entitled to their own happiness, with relatively marginal concern for the happiness of others, no amount of factual argument about the empirical nature of human life—of membership—will lead to a change of mind. Similarly, the social worker who thinks and believes that the development

185

of people as individuals is the irreducible human process after birth will continue to suggest that individuals, groups, and communities should be viewed in terms of single things.

Beliefs about the spiritual/psychological nature of human life are more credible, not less so, when they can be justified in factual terms as well. This is the situation in the case of membership. While there is a difference between the claim that persons are members and the opinion that they ought to behave like members—which is usually thought to mean behaving lovingly and caringly—the ultimate question really is this: Can people ever not behave as members? The answer is clearly no, since membership is basic to all forms of human existence, without regard to its quality.

The plaint that human beings, when viewed as individuals, do not always behave like members is, and ought to be, doomed. All people behave like members because they are members. No person can be an individual and a member at the same time because boundaries between and among people are not closed, nor are they indiscriminately open.

Membership does make room for the celebration of the integrity and autonomy of each human being, while it simultaneously recognizes the fact that this very same integrity and autonomy are social products that result from being permanently linked to one or more persons beyond oneself. There is, therefore, a profound contradiction at work in an individualism that relegates membership to election, to a matter of choice, when the facts indicate the opposite.

The social worker who holds fast to the preeminence of the individual also sees the individual as the building block to the group. All other aspects of human interaction continue to be viewed as the splitoff environment, a distant "surround." These views are not in accord with the facts of human life, even if, for reasons ranging from the theological to the economic, they constitute the preferred mode of thought and action.

If, as was shown in the first chapter of this book, one cannot get the human being beyond the rigid, privatized, and overdetermined boundaries of individualism, a true sense of community becomes impossible. As soon as these boundaries are no longer totally rigid, however, other elements come into play. They invade the heretofore shut off, bounded "I" and allow for the social "we," for the sociality of all human existence.

If the preoccupation with the individual makes the recognition of the community problematic, idealization of the community for its own sake also needs to be avoided. The community is capable of cruelty, totalitarianism, and genocide. It does not help to celebrate the benign community while ignoring its venal possibilities. A community with a destructive ethic is dangerous; it overwhelms its members and destroys some of them through the power of an unbridled and unchecked state. Yet it is unquestionably better to recognize the helplessness of some of the members in the face of discrimination than to pretend that communities exist only in good times. When taken by itself, community is a reasonably neutral concept, as is membership. One discovers their real meanings in the adjectives that describe their qualities.

The relationship between community and membership is reinforcing. Both contain the other. Thus, the relationship is circular in nature, and it is compelling. The compelling aspect is found in the fact that community and membership are means and ends. The end of any community is found in the fact that it exists for its own sake, for without membership there is also no life, social or otherwise. Community is the irreducible quality of biological, social, psychological, symbolic existence. These dimensions give community and membership their general meaning. Their specific meaning is survival, which, among other ways, expresses itself as hope for a better future. In operational as well as ideal terms, this hope is realized in the reality of membership. That is, while it is the nature of all persons that they are members, the members decide upon the qualities of what nature provides.

In sum, whether benign or harmful, community is the medium of life, regardless of the events and processes that determine its quality. The sense of quality of any given community is not absolute but depends on common values, the historical experience of its members and, finally, the perceptions of what ultimately awaits each human being they cherish.

THE IRREDUCIBLE MEMBER

It is instructive to pretend, for the sake of argument, that membership is a matter of choice because that pretense allows us to specify what membership demands. It demands (1) recognition that there are others in the world; (2) recognition that all are interdependent with others; and (3) the ability and willingness to move beyond one's own, separate self.

The recognition of others in the world, the interdependence of the human being, and the willingness to move beyond oneself do not need to be created when one thinks in terms of membership. All three are givens, are aspects of the natural order of human life. One's willingness in this regard is quite irrelevant.

The focus of attention in the argument presented here is not on whether there should be membership. The sole concern is with the qualities of membership as, for example, they are reflected in the division and distribution of resources. This quality was noted in the discussion of social policy as human behavior in Chapter 7. Feelings of alienation, of isolation from others, withdrawal, antisocial behavior are all membership qualities because they involve the self and others at the same time. It is particularly important to understand this central aspect of membership when the subjective experiences these behaviors describe sound as if the person has literally withdrawn from others and is no longer a constituent part of group or society. The questions demanding answers that these feelings pose, however, are these: *About whom* is it that the member does not care? *By whom* is he or she not cared for? *Toward whom and what* is he or she hostile? The answer to all of these questions is always one or many members, including the actor as self. *What the concept of membership suggests is that the member is universal, that all human life, in some way and in some form, is the life of the member.*

In essence, the point to be kept in the forefront of awareness is that whatever clients bring to social workers, and whatever social workers offer to clients, always has social content. Whatever it is, it is offered and accepted by members. Thus, the fact of membership as a natural phenomenon is beyond question. The qualities of membership, however, engage constant attention. The social work task is to render aid in the improved and improvable management of membership.

In social work practice, the members are both clients and social workers. This places social work in the middle of daily life. It means that whatever it is that members experience, whether they bring it to the social worker or not, has impact on other members. And it is in this sense that social work is an expression of what membership means and what it can offer by way of changing behavior to improve its quality.

Thus, not only is membership a central issue for all human beings, it is also the irreducible one.

THE UNIVERSALITY OF MEMBERSHIP IN SOCIAL WORK PRACTICE

In a field as broadly conceived as social work, it is inevitable that specialized practice will evolve spontaneously. It is also logical to expect that specialization makes for expertise in a given problem area in which a social worker is engaged and about which he or she knows more than other social workers not specialized in the same way. Nevertheless, the fact of specialization tends to obscure common themes. When practice is interdisciplinary, for example, it is likely that the social worker will identify more with the dominant professional person on the team—often a physician—than with his or her own profession's core ideas and commitments. Yet membership and the rendering of aid in the management of membership can temper this and similar tendencies because it is the core of social work, regardless of the social worker's specialization. The concept of membership itself, and the definition of social work, is sufficiently general to render the profession a sharp and clear profile, so that blurring with other professions is more readily avoided than heretofore. And it is on this basis that it also becomes easier to entertain and understand the role of specialization without loss of clarity about what is central to all of social work.

This point has been documented in many ways in the preceding chapters. Examples from a variety of social work practice have been cited. How one can, with minor variations, build a systematically organized series of subject areas that help the social worker learn to understand something about the client as a member was demonstrated through a discussion of the dimensions for assessment making. Countertransference management was shown to be necessary in all of social work practice, without regard to specialization, field of practice, or setting. Indeed, it was suggested that the management of countertransference articulates an aspect of the conscious use of self, of the disciplined practice of social work. In all cases, the same formulation of membership is needed simply because all of the people involved in social work practice, including social workers, are members.

The most telling result of the fact that all clients are members is that all behavior must be understood to have consequences, not for the behaving client alone, but for others as well. The dividing line between the client and others is not absolute by any means, and although accessibility from the one to the other is conditional, that is, selective, it is nevertheless constant. This is the reason that the old concept of self-determination requires modification to social self-determination. The client is a social being, a member, a person with connections.

While it may be argued that there is a certain amount of danger in the relative accessibility of persons to each other, there is also protection, provided one views the human condition in terms other than Hobbes' *bellum omnium contra omnes,* "the war of all against all" (Hobbes, 1950). But it is true that the open person, the accessible person, is both the source and recipient of whatever is exchanged. In other words, membership is as potentially dangerous as it is reassuring. The accessibility that allows for affection, aid, and helpfulness permits injury, rejection, and damage. In this sense, membership is risky. It is a risk parents and teachers know. It is one that any person who protects other human beings understands well.

The common knowledge that the human world is reassuring and dangerous at the same time implies that the notion of membership is grasped far more widely than is commonly recognized. And it is a source of some wonder that despite this common knowledge, the language that describes human life—individualism—at least in Western society is still considered appropriate for the reality of human life. The cultural fantasy is that each person is sovereign, with the result that in both good times and bad the individual is considered self-determining and held self-responsible. Not only is this idea deeply rooted in some versions of the democratic, political state, but also in certain versions of Western religion. The point to be noted is that aside from scientifically definable attributes of human life, cultural determinants play their role—and not always in harmony with the facts.

MEMBERSHIP AND METHOD

The traditional division of social work methodology into case-work, group work, community organization, administration, social planning, and research no longer appears adequate. Membership work simultaneously calls attention to each member, while always implying other members. Thus, the membership perspective fits in the center of the social work continuum with the individual at one end and the collectivity at the other. It integrates the major elements that characterize both into one new construct.

Yet membership method is not merely the integration of the traditional methods into a single new one. *The real integration does not take place at the methods level, but rather at the level of understanding human behavior. It is here that the holistic concept of membership is empirically verifiable.*

Membership method replaces the notion that there is such a thing as "a case" or "a group" or "a community" and that one works with "it." All of these traditional concepts tend toward a drastic overdetermination of boundaries. Moreover, none of the three meet the standard of science that holds that boundaries are semipermeable, governed by the principle of selectivity, and accessible by one unit to another, whether that unit be a cell, a conversation, a symbol, or a personality. Because the causes of personal and other problems, conditions, or situations are never individual but are, in fact, social, the resolution, or at least the attempt to resolve them, must employ a view of human behavior that takes these social causes into account. Finally, the social worker does not intervene in a case, or in a group, or in a community. The social worker intervenes in the lives of human beings among other human beings.

THE MEMBERSHIP ATTITUDE

The membership attitude is defined as the willing, as well as the habitual, way of thinking and behaving that views both the self and the other as a continuous process. While both the self and the other are distinct entities, persons with their own identity, history, and future, the membership attitude implies the ability to understand that it is the interdependence of human beings that produces their distinctiveness.

On a conscious level, the membership attitude emphasizes people-hood, community, and ethnic identity (rather than separateness), and boundedness. From the social work standpoint, justice rather than charity is the key term. Social justice addresses those qualitative and quantitative goods to which members are entitled because they are members. Social justice rejects the idea that it is only the well-to-do who are responsible for giving charitably to the poor, whether by voluntary donation or mandatory taxation. Simultaneously, it underlines taking account of the fact that membership under conditions of social justice implies obligation.

Voluntary charity meets mere minimum, if not minimal, standards. Similarly, the payment of taxes to support social welfare efforts under the threat of punishment for failure to do so is only minimally acceptable. Giving out of a sense of justice, on the other hand, is the taking of responsibility for doing what is just. Giving in this sense mixes the giver and the recipient and clearly reflects desirable norms of membership. Nor must giving always be monetary. Giving can be a matter of monitoring one's speech, of attending to the sick, of visiting the isolated, of walking a child to school and taking him or her home again.

The principle involved in the membership attitude is the principle of reciprocity. It suggests that to give voluntarily is more worthy of esteem than to give under compulsion. It also rejects the notion that the poor have so little that they can only receive in order to balance out the deprivation that accounts for the need. Instead, this aspect of the membership attitude holds that even the poorest are entitled to the honor and respect, of self and others, that accrues when one is held worthy enough to have something that one can give to others, even when that something is simply something of oneself.

The membership attitude supplies much of the moral justification and explanation for the quality of membership that accords with the best that is implicit in human life. It is this, in the long run, that every social worker looks for, that he or she expects each client to learn through the process of obtaining help. It is this ability to make the very best of one's memberships that ought to be what clients obtain from the social worker's interventions, transfer to their relationships with others, and utilize long after the social work is done. This is what social work, in the ultimate sense, is all about.

REFERENCES

Hobbes, T. (1950). *Leviathan* (New American ed.). New York: E.P. Dutton.

Index